Before the show – hot seats await the fashion mafia.

CATWALK

INSIDE THE WORLD OF THE SUPERMODELS

CATWALK

INSIDE THE WORLD OF THE **SUPERMODELS**

Sandra Morris

Weidenfeld & Nicolson
London

CATWALK

Left: Helena Christensen photographed by Pamela Hanson on location in Morocco.

Supermodels are a new breed of celebrity who have eclipsed pop stars and movie stars as today's modern icons. Today, such models as Naomi Campbell and Claudia Schiffer are household names whereas, only a decade ago, models were anonymous outside the circuit. These superstars have expanded their careers beyond the runways, as modelling has given them the recognition required to conquer the world. The new renaissance models are astute business women, having built their names into international brands and multi-million-dollar empires.

In 1988, Linda Evangelista and Cindy Crawford were the very first members of the supermodel species to explode onto the circuit. Shortly after, Naomi Campbell, Christy Turlington and Tatjana Patitz united with the original duo. The famous five had arrived! A year or so later, Linda, Christy and Naomi formed The Trinity: the most sought-after trio on the planet, who would pose, parade and hang out together. But the supertroupe were soon joined by Claudia, Helena, Yasmin, Stephanie et al. Then came the second generation of supermodels, headed by Kate Moss. And now a fresh breed of newcomers are emerging, as models like Trish Goff and, more recently, Jodie Kidd enter the supermodel kingdom.

The phrase 'supermodel' was coined by the media, but what triggered this phenomenon? According to Chris Owen, Elite Premier's managing director, it was a combination of factors: 'At that time, Hollywood was lacking glamour, so the media turned its attention to models.' Elite were

The famous five.

instrumental in launching the supermodel. They represented most of the original supermodel pack, and negotiated the first major 'endorsement' contracts. 'It was also the million-dollar cosmetic campaigns,' continues Owen, 'along with Linda Evangelista's infamous comment "we won't get out of bed for less than $10,000", that lifted models into a different sphere.'

To fit into the exclusive supermodel bracket originally required that a model earned in excess

The Fashion Cafe trio. From left, Naomi, Elle and Claudia at the official opening of their New York restaurant.

of a million dollars a year. But today's biggest names are reputed to earn up to twelve million dollars annually. Nowadays, the title is far more freely applied. The word 'super' has become a prefix to virtually anything associated with the model industry, hence superwaifs, superbabes, supermales and superagents.

THE MODEL MAKERS

Supermodels owe much of their glory to a number of modelling's most powerful people: the model agents who discover them; top fashion photographers, designers and editors who give them their big breaks; and the entourage of make-up artists and hair stylists who create their supermodel looks. Without all of these professionals a model would not have a career.

SUPERMODEL MERCHANDISE

Magazines and advertisers have been quick to realize the tremendous pulling power of the supermodel. Supermodels sell. A well-known face can increase a magazine's issue sales by thousands, or help promote a fragrance or fashion line. Companies such as Revlon, Pepsi and Clairol pay a model millions of dollars to endorse their brands and products. Supermodels clearly have commercial clout: whatever they touch turns to gold.

Now, supermodel paraphernalia has swept the world, with collector cards, school books, dolls and posters available. And recently the Elite model agency, in conjunction with its supermodels, has even launched a supermodel fashion line – *Elite Model Fashions*.

CELEBRITIES

Supermodels host chat shows, write for magazines, organize fund-raising events, take cameo roles in movies and, when they are not busy launching calendars and fitness videos, open up their own restaurants.

Like pop and film celebrities, supermodels are pursued by fans from all over the world. Their agents are inundated with mail every week. To satisfy these admirers, some supermodels have produced documentary-style films or books – autobiographies and photographic retrospectives of their modelling careers.

THE MODEL INDUSTRY

The cult of the supermodel has helped turn modelling into a multicultural profession, as girls from far-flung corners of the globe now see it as a respectable and glamorous career. Asian, Eastern European, African

The fall: Naomi Campbell tumbles onto the runway in twelve-inch platforms at the Vivienne Westwood show.

and South American models are now as desirable as their Western counterparts.

Media exposure has raised the profile of modelling and exposed it to criticism from those who want to tarnish its glossy image. Modelling, like any other business where the stakes are high, can be tough, competitive and cut-throat. But according to many models and agents, including April Ducksbury, who has worked in the business for thirty years, it is still a great world to be involved in. 'For the right people, with the right qualities and attitude, it is a wonderful profession with immense opportunity,' says April, partner in top agency Models 1.

The boom in the model industry has created a diverse marketplace for a variety of models. Male modelling is a relatively new area, but a fast expanding one. Mature models are also on the rise, as older women such as fifties model Carmen and famous sixties model Lauren Hutton are enjoying a revival.

PRESS

Rarely a day goes by without newspapers featuring a story about a model's latest beau, movie part, book launch, or any scandal the press can find to write about. Even when Naomi Campbell fell over on the runway at the Vivienne Westwood show it made headline news. The twelve-inch platform shoes have become celebrity memorabilia, and are now on display at London's Victoria & Albert museum. Some journalists put supermodels up on pedestals, and others knock them down. But like most stars, they know their fame comes at a price.

WHAT NEXT?

The flight of the supermodel phenomenon has by no means reached its zenith. Each new generation of supermodels will continue to reach greater and greater heights, and take supermodeldom soaring into the new millennium.

Megastars: Linda Evangelista and George Michael.

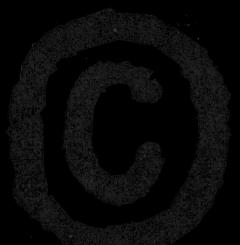

Naomi: the supermodel, the singer, and now the author.

Pleased with the product! Claudia promoting one of her bestselling calendars.

Helena's
signature makes
a fan's day.

Kate's
showcase.

Linda creates
a stir posing
as a plastic
mannequin in
the window of
Harvey Nichols
for a shoot
for Vogue.

VOGUE

V O G U E

FASHIONS

OSEN WITH A MAN IN MIND

VS ABOUT SHOES

ADVANCE
RETAIL

A BRIEF HISTORY OF MODELLING

From the very first mannequins and print-girls to today's supermodels, the 20th century has seen modelling rise to prominence and develop into a thriving industry.

It was shortly after the turn of the century that some of the first print-girls (as photographic models were then known) appeared in magazines such as American and British *Vogue* and *Harper's Bazaar*. Actresses and debutantes were the types of ladies who would pose in the studios of eminent photographers, when they were not busy treading the boards or attending social engagements. These models would be required to hold rigid poses, often for hours at a time.

The inauguration of *haute couture* paved the way for the first show mannequins who modelled expensive evening gowns for the designers' exclusive clientele. From the 1920s onwards, couturiers such as Coco Chanel hired well-bred society girls to model their latest collections for the press, buyers and private customers. These original show mannequins were demure, refined creatures who possessed elegance and poise. In between parading gracefully around the salon, house models would be used for 'fittings'. Models had to fit the designers' specific measurements and would have to stand for several hours, while samples were fitted, pinned and tacked onto their bodies.

To recruit models, photographers and fashion houses had to advertise, specifying the measurements and kind of model they required. In an attempt to supply this demand, a spate of so-called agencies run by undignified individuals suddenly sprang up. But most did nothing but taint the image of the modelling profession.

The first reputable UK model agency, Lucie Clayton's, opened in 1928. Founded as a modelling and grooming school, Clayton's went on to establish itself as a highly successful agency representing well-known models such as Jean Shrimpton, Sandra Paul, Fiona Campbell-Walter, Tania Mallet and Celia Hammond. Young ladies would enrol on a course, learn the fundamental rules of deportment and grooming, and graduate onto the agency's books. On the other side of the Atlantic, the first American models were beginning to emerge from the legendary Ford agency.

Ford was launched from the home of Eileen and Jerry Ford in New York in 1946 and is now run by their daughter Katie. Eileen Ford is known as the godmother of modelling. Unlike her predecessors, she had a far more motherly and professional approach towards the business. Ford handled the careers of some of the earliest successful mannequins, such as Suzy Parker, and later went on to represent many premier-league models including Lauren Hutton, Jerry Hall and Christie Brinkley. In Paris, a third woman

*Left, 1948 cover of American Vogue by Irving Penn, courtesy Vogue, The Condé Nast Publications, UK. **Above**, Jean Shrimpton by Cecil Beaton, 1964 .*

joined the female agents. Dorian Leigh, who had been a successful American model, started up The Fashion Bureau – the first French model agency. These agents were kept busy arranging diaries to fit in around their models' high society lifestyles.

The 1960s brought infinite change to the modelling scene. With the strong influence of fashion and pop music on this exciting new era, the model industry was hungry for fresh faces. And so a new breed of model girl was created: the sixties hippy chick. These new models were not like the mechanical, poised models of previous decades; they were energetic and animated, cavorting freely around the studio in the funky new fashions.

While Mary Quant was designing the mini, photographer David Bailey was busy discovering Jean Shrimpton (known as The Shrimp), dating her, and turning her into a star. Her wide-eyed gaze and child-like innocence was to embody the sophisticated end of sixties fashion. This decade also spawned names like Veruschka and Lauren Hutton. However, it was Leslie Hornby, alias Twiggy, who became a household name and captured the attention of the world. Under the guidance of her Svengali, Justin de Villeneuve, she rose to the top and became a larger-than-life icon. Her elfin face, wide eyes and stick-thin body combined with her cockney accent were to reflect the quintessential mood of the swinging sixties. Although her modelling career only lasted four years, during that time she became so well-known that she was able to market her name into a brand. There was a Twiggy hair dressing salon, hosiery range and London boutique. Models were no longer nameless clothes horses – they had become as marketable as the clothes they were selling.

In the 1960s a model's career only spanned a few years – a decade if they were lucky. And as Leslie Kark, owner of Lucie Clayton points out, even the famous models earned far less in a year than the current supermodels earn in a day: 'In the sixties top models earned at most £10 to £12 an hour, and would usually work between three to four days a week,' says Leslie. At the end of their short-lived career, some models went on to 'marry well', and others, like Lauren Hutton and Joanna Lumley, became accomplished actresses. Jean Shrimpton moved to the English countryside to run a hotel and Veruschka became an artist.

Above, Lucie Clayton teaches her protégées the art of deportment. *Right*, print-girl Twiggy.

The 1970s witnessed the demise of the Lucie Clayton agency (although the school is still running) and the birth of what was to become the largest and most powerful agency network in the world – Elite. John Casablancas opened the very first Elite office in Paris in 1971. As the fashion trade expanded, modelling grew into a large industry. But in contrast to the notorious sixties, the models of the next two decades were to keep a comparatively low profile. Jerry Hall, Marie Helvin and Christie Brinkley were three of the very few prominent names of this era.

Up until the mid 1980s, modelling was split into two main divisions: show and photographic. Show models were tall sylph-like creatures who had strong angular features and a penchant for sauntering down the catwalk. The main requirement for these models was that they walked well and had mastered their pivots and turns. They also needed make-up skills, as in those days models were often required to do their own hair and make-up.

A photographic model would need to be photogenic as well as have the right height and vital statistics. And as the emphasis moved away from formal poses, a model had to be able to move well and be spontaneous in front of the camera. Models would usually specialize in one area of work. Today however, most models work in all fields of high fashion modelling, including catwalk, commercials, videos and photographic work for fashion magazines and advertising campaigns.

By the start of the 1980s there was a boom in the fashion industry and, as more fashion, fragrance and cosmetic clients grasped the powerful concept of advertising, the demand for models increased accordingly. Campaigns went pan-European and then the industry turned global. Elite and Ford opened branches in all the fashion capitals of the world and large independent agencies began springing up everywhere. Then came the biggest and most important factor that was to revolutionize the model industry – the birth of the supermodel.

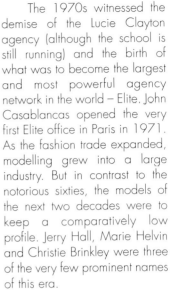

*Above, The Picnic, by Cecil Beaton, 1965, with Jean Shrimpton and Celia Hammond. **Left**, Jerry Hall, 1980.*

13

BRUNI
CARLA

UK AGENCY: **STORM**

NEW YORK AGENCY: **WOMEN**

PARIS AGENCY:

THE MARILYN AGENCY

NATIONALITY: **ITALIAN**

HEIGHT: **5'9½"**

HAIR: **BROWN**

EYES: **BLUE**

VOGUE

AUG
£2.50

Rifat Ozbek: sultan of style

Helena Christensen at home

Mommie dearest: does she expect too much?

The new silhouette

First look

Catwalk guide to a great season

9 770262 213029

QUEEN OF ELEGANCE

It was the delicate blend of a porcelain complexion and startling blue eyes, combined with her elegant stance that sent the fashion world into a spin. Today, Carla is one of the most coveted models in the world. Her face has been enshrined on the covers of almost every fashion magazine, including many editions of *Vogue*, *Elle*, and *Marie Claire*. She has been photographed by the great masters such as Steven Meisel, Patrick Demarchelier and Pamela Hanson, and has sashayed down the runways for every top international designer. Add to that a score of advertising campaigns, including Christian Dior, Escada Couture, Iceberg, Blumarine and Prada, and it comes as no surprise that this consummate professional is one of modelling's highest earners.

PROFESSIONAL

It is not only the photogenic qualities of this Italian supermuse that photographers and fashion editors remark on: she has charisma and treats every job with the utmost professionalism. 'I love working with Carla,' says top photographer Pamela Hanson. 'She is smart, with a great sense of humour and is always a very hard worker.'

ARISTOCRAT

Carla Bruni was born in Turin into a wealthy, aristocratic Italian family. When she was five years old

her parents moved the family to Paris to avoid the Red Brigade kidnappers that were prevalent in Italy at that time. Carla spent many of her childhood years at boarding school in Switzerland. Then, after completing school, she moved back to France to study art and architecture at the University of Paris. Carla inherited her artistic flair from her parents, both accomplished musicians. Her future was carved out for her – until her brother's girlfriend suggested that Carla tried modelling. The first Paris agency she approached could see that this exquisite nineteen-year-old creature had the face and body to make a fortune.

RETREAT

When she is not trekking around the globe Carla resides in her penthouse in Paris, or escapes to her favourite retreat: her family's Art Deco villa in Saint Tropez. Here, she spends time relaxing with her French lawyer boyfriend, Arno Klarsfeld, or entertaining celebrity friends. Helmut Newton, Robert De Niro and Clint Eastwood are among the well-known guests who have spent time at Carla's beachside home.

Carla is a supermodel *extraordinaire* and, with her aristocratic beauty, eccentricity and celebrity lifestyle, is a role model for many women. Reported by the media to have a reputedly red hot love life, she now receives the kind of press coverage usually reserved for royalty. ©

NEW YORK AGENCY: **FORD**

PARIS AGENCY: **FORD**

NATIONALITY: **AMERICAN**

HEIGHT: **5'10"**

HAIR: **BROWN**

EYES: **GREEN**

CHRISTY

TURLINGTON

THE RISE

At the tender age of thirteen Christy was spotted by a photographer whilst taking part in a local gymkhana. After an initial photo session she was signed up by a small San Francisco model agency and began occasionally working on minor assignments during her holidays. Then fate intervened when she was brought to the attention of the godmother of modelling – Eileen Ford. Eileen had been shown a rather amateur photograph of Christy, but nevertheless was struck by her strong bone structure and large innocent eyes. Once with Ford, Christy was in constant demand but, determined to finish her studies, waited until she was eighteen before launching into modelling full time.

ACCOLADES

With her classic features, Christy embodies the kind of timeless beauty that the fashion world never tires of. During her career, she has scooped some of the industry's premier assignments, graced the covers of the glossies and received one of modelling's highest accolades: a major cosmetics contract for Calvin Klein's *Eternity* fragrance. She has also featured in advertising campaigns for Maybelline and Shiseido. Christy has built a reputation for being one of the most charming and down-to-earth supermodels. It is this refreshing attitude, coupled with her willingness to muck-in on shoots, that has top photographers and fashion editors so enamoured of her.

In the midst of supermodel stardom, Christy (nicknamed Turlie) found time to make a movie about her career. The documentary, *Christy Turlington Backstage*, followed her life during the Spring 1994 collections.

VENTURES

Between cavorting around studios and treading the runways, Christy has found time to support good causes and is currently an activist for animal rights. She has donated her time to working with Peta – one of the leading animal rights organizations. In 1993, a naked photograph of Christy hit the billboards in a powerful anti-fur campaign. She recently produced her own calendar that was shot in El Salvador – her mother's native country – and generously donated a large proportion of the profits to the El Salvadoran Foundation. In a less serious venture, Christy joined forces with the Fashion Cafe trio and also invested in a jazz club and restaurant with her younger sister Erin. The Up and Down Club has become one of San Francisco's hippest night spots.

FACE OF THE CENTURY

Christy was awarded the title *The Face of the 20th Century* by New York's Metropolitan Museum of Art. They paid her another tribute in 1993 when they displayed over a hundred mannequins in her likeness. She has been hailed as one of the most beautiful women of our time; however, her astonishing career cannot be attributed to her looks alone, but also to her intelligence and positive attitude to modelling. ©

BY KELLY KLEIN COURTESY VOGUE. THE CONDÉ NAST PUBLICATIONS, UK

CINDY CRAWFORD

UK AGENCY: **ELITE PREMIER**

NEW YORK AGENCY: **ELITE**

PARIS AGENCY: **ELITE**

NATIONALITY: **AMERICAN**

HEIGHT: **5'9½"**

HAIR: **BROWN**

EYES: **BROWN**

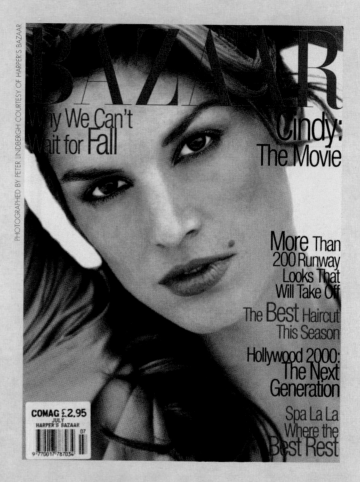

TRADEMARK

The All-American glamour girl was born and raised in the countryside of Illinois, USA. At seventeen, Cynthia Ann left her small home town of Dekalb and headed for the bright lights of Chicago to break into the world of modelling. Her first attempts were unsuccessful: agencies refused to take her on unless she removed the prominent mole above her lip. Despite rejection, Cindy was not prepared to alter her face to suit the whims of a few model agents, and she continued to be headstrong, doing the rounds of agencies. Eventually she approached Elite, who succumbed to her charm and beauty and immediately took Cindy – mole included – onto their books. Her birthmark soon became her trademark. The rest is history.

It all started to happen for Cindy in 1986 when she became a finalist in Elite's Model Look contest and moved from Elite Chicago to New York. This coquettish beauty with the impossibly glossy image and perfectly formed features soon became one of the world's most sought-after models. Cindy has been photographed by the best: Patrick Demarchelier, Richard Avedon, Peter Lindbergh, Herb Ritts, Bruce Weber and Annie Leibowitz, to name but a few. She has starred in high-profile advertisements, including a major Pepsi campaign, and was also the first top model to step daringly over the boundaries of fashion modelling by posing nude for *Playboy* in 1988.

SPOKESPERSON

In 1989 Cindy landed a major cosmetics contract. Described by Victor Skrebneski (photographer and mentor from her early modelling days) as the 'million-dollar face' she was the ideal representative for Revlon, and was contracted to promote them worldwide, not only as a model but as a spokesperson. 'She radiates a certain happiness that is at the heart of true beauty and our philosophy,' says George Fellows, president of Revlon worldwide.

CAREER WOMAN

Cindy is head of the million-dollar industry she has built around her name. She has released two of the most successful fitness videos, *Shape Your Body* and *The Next Challenge*, and launched a jewellery line. Cindy's swimwear calendars, from which she donates half of the profits to the children's leukaemia foundation, have also become best sellers. Her career certainly does not lack variety. She hosts *House of Style* (an MTV chat show) and, after a three month crash course in acting, made her debut in Joel Silver's movie *Fair Game*. She has also signed a two-picture deal with Warner Brothers.

FAME

Cindy has become a household name. When she first married Hollywood heart-throb Richard Gere, it was Gere's career that benefited from being on the arm of Cindy. The first to be fêted as a supermodel, she even had a song, 'Cindy C', dedicated to her by Prince.

Today, at the peak of her powers, Cindy Crawford is the very epitome of a superstar model: an absolute professional, an international personality and an exceptionally astute business woman. ©

CLAUDIA

SCHIFFER

BARDOT-ESQUE

Claudia Schiffer has been described as 'unparalleled' and called 'the most beautiful girl in the world' by *GQ* magazine. Her glamorous, sex-kitten appeal has often led to her being compared to Bardot and Monroe. But this modern-day beauty has become a legendary icon in her own right. More celebrity than supermodel, Claudia has been featured on the covers of *Rolling Stone* and *Vanity Fair* and has even been entertained by heads of state.

FAIRY TALE

Claudia grew up in Rheinburg, Germany. Her father was a lawyer and keen for Claudia, his eldest child, to continue the family's profession. But her father's hopes were dashed when, at the age of seventeen, she was discovered in a Düsseldorf discotheque by two presidents from the top Paris model agency, Metropolitan. Claudia moved to Paris, and in a very short time was enjoying unrivalled success.

Ellen von Unwerth was one of the first to spot Claudia's enormous potential and to photograph her for the highly acclaimed Guess? campaign. Her Bardot pout and vampish looks fitted in perfectly with the image of both the fragrance and the jeans. From there she hit the big time. Claudia now holds the record for appearing on more magazine covers (over 400) than any other model in history.

CHANEL

Fashion doyen Karl Lagerfeld had seen Claudia on a Herb Ritts photograph for British *Vogue*: 'I immediately noticed a star quality: far more than what is needed for a good model', comments Lagerfeld. He hired her for the January 1990 Chanel couture show – her debut runway performance. Not surprisingly, she was very nervous. But this made no difference to Lagerfeld, who adored Claudia and chose to make her his muse for the great house of Chanel. Since then her mentor has become a great friend. 'She is a star – independent from her photographic and runway work. Wherever she goes, she is the centre of attention, like movie stars of the past,' Karl Lagerfeld enthuses.

FAN CLUB

Goddess of the modelling world, Claudia Schiffer is adored by fans from around the globe. She receives over 3000 letters each week. To the delight of her devoted fan club, she has written her autobiography,

entitled *Memories*. She has also been immortalized on film in a documentary directed by Nicolas Racheline, that aimed to answer her admirers' many questions. Claudia, alongside supermodels Naomi and Elle, was responsible for launching The Fashion Cafe. Away from the modelling scene, Claudia likes to spend time with special friends. Magician David Copperfield has occupied much of her time since he plucked her out of the audience at one of his shows. Her Paris agent, Arline Souliers, sums her up perfectly, 'This girl has a very special karma . . . everything she touches turns to gold.' ©

| UK AGENCY: **ELITE PREMIER** |
| NEW YORK AGENCY: **METROPOLITAN** |
| PARIS AGENCY: **METROPOLITAN** |

| NATIONALITY: **GERMAN** |
| HEIGHT: **5'11"** |
| HAIR: **BLONDE** |
| EYES: **BLUE** |

MACPHERSON

ELLE

UK AGENCY: **STORM**
NEW YORK AGENCY: **WOMEN**
MILAN AGENCY: **CITY**

NATIONALITY: **AUSTRALIAN**
HEIGHT: **6'**
HAIR: **BROWN**
EYES: **BROWN**

model agency. Then, en route back to Sydney after a skiing holiday in Colorado, Elle dropped into the New York model agency affiliated with her agency back home. The agency – who were enthralled by her looks – begged her not to get on her return flight. She didn't, and after a decade of swimwear shoots, catwalk shows and magazine covers, she joined the glittering galaxy of supermodels.

ENTREPRENEUR

Elle has branched out from modelling and turned her stunning physical assets into a multimillion dollar empire: Elle Macpherson Inc. It began with a lingerie mail-order company, Elle Macpherson Intimates, which is now Australia's number-one-selling lingerie line with a reported yearly turnover of 30 million dollars. Elle is the total woman. A sex kitten who, after appearing on the cover of Sports Illustrated, also represents an image of vitality. This led to Elle launching two fitness videos, including her most recent Elle Macpherson – The Body Workout. She also produces annual calendars and has appeared in her own ESPN2 TV show, Hot Summer Nights. Her appetite for enterprising ventures, along with her compulsive drive, led to Elle becoming one of the three supermodels behind The Fashion Café.

SIREN

Elle has also very successfully dabbled in acting. Her first starring on-screen was in the box office hit Sirens, where she played one of the Australian artist Norman Lindsay's nude models. She has since completed two other movies – Jane Eyre and If Lucy Fell – and has signed a major contract with Miramax Films.

Today, she resides in New York, but likes to spend time in her native Australia. From boardroom to catwalk, Elle successfully juggles her career as a supermodel, actress and business woman, the best is yet to come from this remarkable superwoman. ©

'THE BODY'

In 1986, Elle Macpherson was dubbed 'The Body' by Time magazine, a nickname that has stayed with her ever since. Standing six-foot in her bare feet, her immense height, 44-inch legs and vital statistics of 36-24-35 has made her the envy of many women and other models alike. In 1994, Playboy magazine – after a great deal of persuasion – convinced Elle to pose nude for a Herb Ritts shoot. Elle, who is completely unselfconscious and uninhibited about her body, handled it with the greatest of ease.

EARLY DAYS

Born Eleanor Gow in Sydney, Australia, Elle grew up by the sea and enjoyed water sports and fitness activities. As a teenager she was the academic type who had never harboured thoughts of modelling and was studying hard for a profession in law. But her career as a lawyer was stymied when at sixteen she blossomed from a gawky adolescent into a tall, statuesque beauty and was signed up by a Sydney

EVA HERZIGOVA

UK AGENCY:	**STORM**
NEW YORK AGENCY:	**METROPOLITAN**
PARIS AGENCY:	**METROPOLITAN**

NATIONALITY:	**CZECH**
HEIGHT:	**5'11"**
HAIR:	**BLONDE**
EYES:	**BLUE**

This arresting beauty with such piercing blue eyes was the ultimate model for what was to become the most talked about advertising campaign of the nineties. The seductive photograph with the provocative 'Hello Boys' slogan increased Triumph's sales by forty-one per cent, proving that Eva has tremendous pulling power. Local authorities in the UK were worried that the ad would be a road safety hazard as her face – and well-endowed cleavage – peered down from billboards and brought traffic to a complete standstill!

RIGHT PLACE — RIGHT TIME

At seventeen years old, Eva Herzigova was whisked from her little town, Letvinov in northern Czech-oslovakia, to the chic boulevards of Paris, unaware that in a few years time she would become one of the most desirable women in the world.

It all began when Eva took a trip with her parents to the capital, Prague. Here, she met up with a friend who had heard that a top Paris agency was in town holding a model contest. Eager to go along herself, her friend urged Eva to accompany her. Eva, who had been daunted by the prospect of being surrounded by beautiful women, entered the contest – and won. Her plans to go to university and study economics abruptly changed as she set off for Paris to begin to work on a lucrative modelling contract.

WONDERGIRL

Eva was working reasonably well until she found herself in front of top photographer Ellen von Unwerth's camera. Ellen photographed Eva for the high-profile Guess? jeans campaign. From then on, Eva added a sparkle that was missing from the pages of glossy magazines and soon gained international status as a top model. But what really propelled her into the superleague was the decision by lingerie giants Triumph to use Eva as their model for the new Wonderbra campaign.

MOVIE STAR

Today, Eva is more of a star than a model. Her vampish looks, baby-fine platinum hair, and curvaceous body have characterized her as the industry's sex goddess. She oozes glamour with her forties film star appeal, and has been likened to Marilyn Monroe. From a young age Eva had dreamt of becoming an actress. Now Hollywood appears to be her next step as she made her debut appearance alongside Gerard Depardieu in Jean-Marie Poire's *Guardian Angels*.

BLIND DATE

Eva is engaged to Tico Torres, drummer for the rock group Bon Jovi. But unlike the usual model-meets-rock-star scenario, this couple met on a blind date. He had no idea she was a supermodel, nor she that he was a famous musician. It was love at first sight. Success has not prevented Eva from keeping her feet firmly on the ground by constantly reminding herself how lucky she is. Jet-setting around the world and enjoying luxurious homes in New York, Paris and Monaco are a far cry from the simple life she left behind. ©

19

HELENA CHRISTENSEN

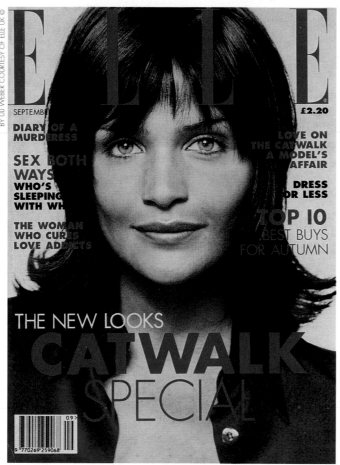

UK AGENCY: SELECT
PARIS AGENCY: THE MARILYN AGENCY

NATIONALITY: DANISH
HEIGHT: 5'9½"
HAIR: DARK BROWN
EYES: GREEN

of the top advertising campaigns. She superseded Linda Evangelista as the Kenar girl, and has appeared in ads for Cover Girl, Hennes, Patrick Cox and Gianni Versace. When British clothing company Dorothy Perkins decided to re-vamp their image, they chose Helena to endorse their name in a major campaign, which covered billboards across the UK. She was also selected as the supermodel to publicize Robert Altman's film *Prêt-à-Porter* . . . Helena, wearing nothing but a smile and a feather boa, peered down from billboards all around the globe.

DECOR
Apart from her love of food, her other great passion in life is interior design, and she enjoys using her artistic talent to decorate her apartments. In her spare time she rummages around antique and second-hand shops looking for those rare artefacts to add to her collection. Helena's Copenhagen apartment is her pride and joy, and was featured in an edition of British *Vogue*.

PHOTOGRAPHER
Modelling has taken Helena to a variety of locations around the world: from the runways of the fashion capitals, to the more primitive locations of Third World countries. When she is on location or travelling for pleasure, Helena enjoys photographing the landscape and indigenous peoples. It is said that she is becoming quite a serious lenswoman.

Helena has been a constant fixture in the gossip columns, especially when she was dating INXS star Michael Hutchence. But she is an undisputed superstar in her own right. Not only is she adored by fans, but is a firm favourite with the media and the fashion world. Top designer John Galliano describes Helena as a real woman. 'Always inspirational, she breathes life and fire into my clothes.' ©

CHILD MODEL
Born in Copenhagen in 1965, Helena inherited her exotic beauty from her Peruvian mother and Danish father. She was modelling even before she could walk or talk and as she grew older, she blossomed into an angelic little girl with the charm and prettiness that made her a popular fixture in magazines all over Europe. For Helena, a career in adult modelling was simply a natural progression. After being accepted by a top Paris agency at eighteen, she left Copenhagen and settled in Paris.

BREAKTHROUGH
Her unique ability to appear mysterious, yet attainable, provoked an instant reaction from modelling's kingpins. Her breakthrough came in the shape of a cover shoot for British *Vogue* with top photographer Peter Lindbergh.

In 1991, her appearance in Chris Isaak's music video *Wicked Game* increased her profile further and cast her as one of the sexiest of the modelling elite. This Inca beauty, never off the covers of *Vogue*, *Elle* and *Harper's Bazaar*, has become 'the face' in many

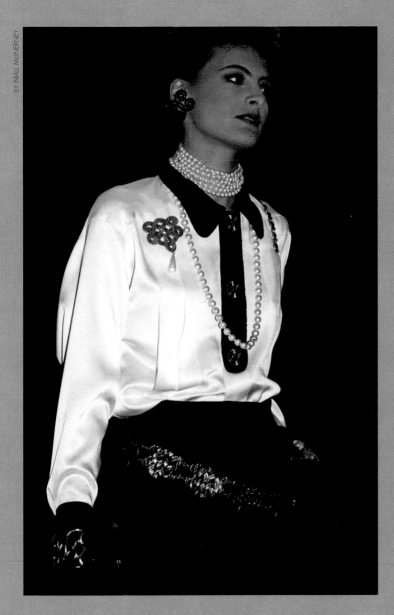

BY NIALL McINERNEY

INÈS DE LA FRESSANGE

NEW YORK AGENCY: **PAULINE'S**
PARIS AGENCY: **PAULINE'S**

NATIONALITY: **FRENCH**
HEIGHT: **5'11"**
HAIR: **BROWN**
EYES: **HAZEL**

MUSE

Inès de la Fressange has a style of her own, a look that symbolizes chic sophistication. It was precisely this that convinced designer Karl Lagerfeld to hire her as his first major muse for the House of Chanel. She would represent Chanel and help to attract a younger customer. This exclusive contract meant she could no longer work for any other fashion house.

BOUTIQUE

Inès' contract with Chanel ended in 1990. It was now time for her to change direction and start work on a new project. Cut out for a career in fashion, Inès had always enjoyed modelling, but was keen to move into the retail side of the business. For the next two years she worked day and night designing her own collection. In 1992, she opened her boutique Inès de la Fressange in a fashionable arrondissement of Paris. The boutique not only houses her collection but also sells unusual artefacts, along with a selection of accessories and shoes. Like Inès, her boutique reflects an image of sheer elegance.

MODERN MANNEQUIN

Born in France in 1959, Inès has lived in that country ever since and now resides in Paris with her husband, Luigi d'Urso, and daughter, Nine. Inès is a great modern mannequin. But today she spends far more time working on her collection and controlling her thriving business than modelling. Although she does make exceptions . . . especially when it comes to modelling her own creations. She recently appeared in a spread for American *Elle*, wearing clothes from her very own label. ©

REJECTED

During her triumphant career Inès de la Fressange has established herself as a well-known name, with her own boutique and international recognition as a famous model. But life wasn't always so glamorous. Inès, who was not conventionally pretty and very different from the girls on the modelling circuit at that time, was rejected by many of the agencies she approached. Eventually a Paris agent spotted her potential and signed her up. 'She had a strong face with an aquiline nose, which was far from the archetypal blue-eyed, button-nosed blonde that was all the rage,' explains her agent, Pauline.

COUP

Although Inès began modelling at fifteen, it was not until she was eighteen that her career took off. She was photographed for French *Elle* by top photographer Paolo Roversi which earned her instant recognition. She went on to work for many of the other glossy magazines and was soon being wooed by leading French fashion houses. Then she achieved her biggest coup – a contract with Chanel.

MULDER

KAREN

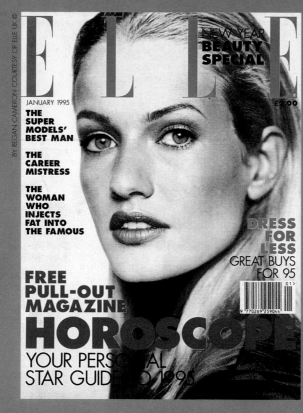

UK AGENCY: **ELITE PREMIER**

NEW YORK AGENCY: **ELITE**

PARIS AGENCY: **ELITE**

NATIONALITY: **DUTCH**

HEIGHT: **5'10"**

HAIR: **BLONDE**

EYES: **GREY-BLUE**

LITTLE DUTCH GIRL

She was born in 1967, in a small village outside The Hague. When Karen was seventeen she was flicking through a magazine with a friend and noticed details of a model contest. Karen, who wore braces and did not think she was particularly pretty, immediately rejected the idea. Little did she know that within a few years she would become a modelling sensation. Unbeknown to Karen, her friend had managed to get hold of a holiday snapshot and entered Karen into Elite's model contest. A few months later a letter arrived inviting Karen to participate in Elite's Look of the Year competition.

The contest was held in Amsterdam and to Karen's complete surprise, she won! She took part in the international finals later that year and, despite taking second place, was invited to fly to Paris and sign a substantial contract with Elite. Karen's parents needed some convincing, but eventually they supported her decision and allowed their somewhat naive, yet excited daughter to head towards her destiny.

BIG BREAK

The fashion world sat up and took notice of her natural beauty. Soon she was working with such highly regarded photographers as Arthur Elgort, Gilles Bensimon and Helmut Newton. Karen's first major feat came when she appeared on the cover of British

Vogue, an achievement that prompted many other commissions including campaigns for Nivea, Synergie, Ralph Lauren, Claude Montana and Guess?. Subsequently, she has graced the covers of almost every fashion magazine, and has become one of modelling's biggest names.

TIMELESS BEAUTY

Karen's appeal is universal. Described by *Vogue* editors as 'a blonde with class', she is blessed with a timeless beauty that, to the delight of the fashion world, metamorphoses into a variety of looks. She can be transformed from a demure blonde into a Marlene Dietrich-style film star or a fresh-faced country girl. On the runways, she is quite as graceful as a gazelle.

HOME

Today, Karen has an apartment in Paris and a seaside home in Monaco to which she retreats when in need of respite from the fashion world. She spends much of her time with her fiancé, Jean-Yves Lefur, who has recently produced a series of television documentaries about Karen and other supermodels, including Claudia Schiffer. In true supermodel style, Karen is planning to launch her own much-awaited video, which profiles her career and reveals her beauty secrets.

FUND RAISING

Karen knows she is very lucky to have made a success of her natural gifts and tries to help those less fortunate than herself. She is involved with helping underprivileged children, and in 1995 bought a château in France and set up a scheme to give those children holidays there. Her ultimate aim is to put the recognition modelling has given her to good use and devote much of her spare time to fund-raising for worthy causes. According to Karen – who has become so famous that she has a tulip named after her – the secret of her success is 'just hard work'. ©

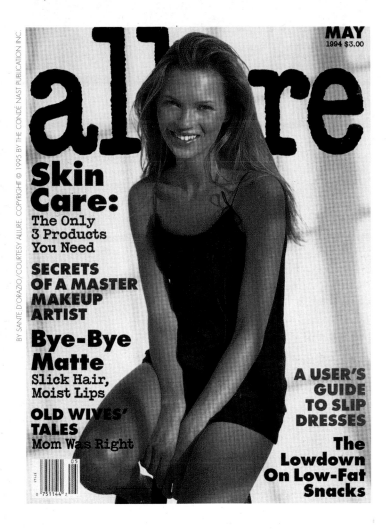

MAY
1994 $3.00

allure

Skin Care:
The Only
3 Products
You Need

**SECRETS
OF A MASTER
MAKEUP
ARTIST**

**Bye-Bye
Matte**
Slick Hair,
Moist Lips

**OLD WIVES'
TALES**
Mom Was Right

**A USER'S
GUIDE
TO SLIP
DRESSES**

**The
Lowdown
On Low-Fat
Snacks**

0 751144

KATE

MOSS

UK AGENCY:	**STORM**
NEW YORK AGENCY:	**WOMEN**
PARIS AGENCY:	**THE MARILYN AGENCY**

NATIONALITY:	**BRITISH**
HEIGHT:	**5'8"**
HAIR:	**LIGHT BROWN**
EYES:	**HAZEL**

Bruce Weber, along with the rest of the heavyweights. Soon, her striking face was to decorate the covers of *Elle*, *Vogue*, *Allure* and *Harper's Bazaar*. Kate was also to be seen on all the top designers' runways, strutting her stuff and holding her own against the taller, more experienced supermodels. Today, Kate remains a favourite of many designers, including John Galliano. 'Kate is a true friend who hasn't changed since the age of fourteen,' says Galliano.

OBSESSION

Photographer Patrick Demarchelier introduced Kate to Calvin Klein in 1992. Soon she became the face of Klein as he made her his muse for both CK apparel and his *Obsession* and *cK one* fragrances. First she was used to promote his underwear range, teamed with rap singer Marky Mark for a memorable advertising campaign. Then came the famously provocative shot of Kate posed naked on a couch. The fragrance: *Obsession*. The photographer: former boyfriend Mario Sorrento. The slogan: 'I love you, Kate'. By now the whole world was obsessed with Kate.

THE PHENOMENON

Kate Moss is a phenomenon. She has become the idol of the nineties for teenagers around the world who can identify with the ordinary yet groovy image that is so evident in both her interviews and photographs. To satisfy her fans, she launched her own book entitled *Kate* – a lavishly illustrated retrospective of her career. In 1995 this super-icon was presented with a very special award – Fashion Personality of the Year.

Originally labelled 'superwaif' and hounded by the press for looking pencil-thin, Kate has now developed a more womanly physique. Aside from modelling, she dabbles in fashion styling, and has enjoyed styling shoots for photographers, as well as a fashion story for the American magazine *Mirabella*. For the time being, Kate is not dwelling on the future, and is taking time to appreciate her well-earned success. ©

PLUCKED FROM OBSCURITY

'Kate is an enigma. It is not only her looks, but her whole personality and aura that have made her so famous,' says Sarah Doukas, managing director of London's Storm model agency. Kate met her destiny at New York's JFK airport in 1988 when, returning to England from a family holiday in the Bahamas, she was spotted by Sarah. 'She had a beautiful face and wonderful bone structure, and I felt very strongly from the moment I set eyes upon her that she was going to be special.' Until the day she was discovered, Kate Moss from Croydon, South London, was like any other fourteen year old school kid.

THE RISE

It all started to happen for Kate after Corinne Day photographed her for *The Face* magazine. Her child-like innocence, coupled with her uncontrived beauty and waif-like frame, embodied the grunge fashion movement. Suddenly, the fashion industry realized Kate was special. Her nonchalant, couldn't-give-a-damn attitude to the business made her stand out from the crowd. This girl was unlike any other model the fashion world had seen. And, at just under 5'8", she was breaking all the rules. Within a matter of weeks, Kate had become the 'Next Big Thing'.

Photographers and fashion editors from all over the world wanted to hire Kate. Steven Meisel photographed her, then Patrick Demarchelier and

EVANGELISTA

LINDA

UK AGENCY:	**ELITE PREMIER**
NEW YORK AGENCY:	**ELITE**
PARIS AGENCY:	**ELITE**
NATIONALITY:	**ITALIAN/CANADIAN**
HEIGHT:	**5'9½"**
HAIR:	**BLONDE**
EYES:	**BLUE-GREEN**

Lindbergh was of paramount importance to her success. Later, her other Pygmalion and now great friend, Steven Meisel noted her new look, photographed her, and catapulted her to the famous supermodel Trinity. Linda imposed herself on the world, and helped redefine the status of the model.

RUNWAY DIVA

Linda has paraded down the international runways for many years and is a firm favourite of all the top designers. Nowadays, she is in the enviable position of picking and choosing for whom she models. Captured on film by the world's leading photographers, including Peter Lindbergh, Patrick Demarchelier, Herb Ritts and Richard Avedon, her face has adorned the covers of almost every glossy magazine. Linda has also starred in countless advertisements for prestigious designers such as Chanel, Dolce & Gabbana and Gianni Versace, to name but a few. More recently, Karl Lagerfeld has used her to represent Chloé, and she has won a major contract as a model and spokesperson with Clairol. She can also be seen in two of George Michael's hit videos: *Freedom 90* and *Too Sexy*.

CHAMELEON

She has been labelled 'The Chameleon' for her unique ability to re-invent herself to meet the constant demands of the fashion industry and is adored by top designers like Gianni Versace for such great versatility. 'I never tire of Linda as she continually changes her look – she can be sexy, innocent, androgynous, play the *femme fatale* as well as the girl next door. This is why I have used her in many press and advertising campaigns,' explains Versace.

PYGMALION

Linda grew up in Ontario, Canada. By the time she was twelve, she had joined a Toronto model agency and was working during her holidays. At sixteen, whilst entering a local beauty contest, she was spotted by a talent scout from Elite. Linda was signed up by Elite New York before moving to Paris to further her career.

Once in Paris, her career started to move in the right direction. But it was not until 1989, when she met photographer Peter Lindbergh, that it reached a turning point. Lindbergh suggested she cut her long silky mane into a short crop: a style that became known as 'the Evangelista look'. Her encounter with

'EVANGELISTA'

Like most dedicated supermodels, Linda spends little time socializing outside the business. So it comes as no surprise that she met her current partner, the star of TV's *Twin Peaks* Kyle McLachlan, during a fashion shoot in New York.

She has not produced her own videos or calendars, nor does she have any acting ambitions. Today, Linda is content with her phenomenal modelling career. By keeping such a high profile she has attracted an immense following, and to the delight of her admirers she is planning to produce a book. *Evangelista* will be an up-tempo work of art that follows her remarkable career. ©

NADJA AUERMANN

PLATINUM

She was an overnight sensation. In October 1993, Nadja Auermann exploded onto the scene from nowhere, taking the Paris collections by storm. The reason? A simple transformation – from a mediocre mousy-haired model to a platinum blonde superstar. She took the plunge and it paid off. She was the girl everyone in the modelling world was talking about.

TREND-SETTER

Her timing was perfect. The waif look was dying and the fashion world was hungry for a stronger image. Nadja symbolized this movement and put glamour back into fashion. Steven Meisel photographed her for American *Vogue*, and shortly afterwards there was a fashion story in *Harper's Bazaar*. British *Vogue's* fashion editor Lucinda Chambers, one of the first to use Nadja before the dramatic change, explains: 'I hired Nadja for a Helmut Newton-style shoot with Ellen von Unwerth. We took over the billiard room in a hotel and no sooner had we arrived when Nadja, clad in nothing but a mask and stilettos, began cavorting around the billiard table. She moved in such a creative way and amazed us all.'

Lucinda was also one of the first to use the new-look Nadja: 'With her white hair and slightly tanned body, her almost unearthly look was perfect for our punk story.' After Nadja appeared in *Vogue*, many other models bleached their hair. Blonde was in!

SPOTTED

Nadja was born and raised in Berlin. She was spotted in a local café by a model scout when she was nineteen years old. As a child, it had never occurred to Nadja to become a model. This girl had other ambitions, which included architecture, furniture design and becoming the Chancellor of Germany!

SUBLIME

When Nadja stalks the runway, her lissom body and two-dimensional image turn into something sublime. She is the ultimate runway mannequin: her haunting beauty and elongated legs have made her the star of every show. Right from the start she created an impact on the influential fashion gurus, and was soon a favourite of Karl Lagerfeld, who uses her to promote his signature collection and fragrance.

PRINT-GIRL

After a new, shorter haircut in September 1994, Nadja achieved what every model dreams of: simultaneous covers of *Harper's Bazaar* and American and British *Vogue*. Subsequently, she illuminated the covers of many magazines and was booked for the illustrious advertising campaigns of Valentino, Lagerfeld, Blumarine, Gianni Versace, Anne Klein, Rochas and Prada.

The teutonic blonde had another surprise in store for the fashion world when, at the Spring/Summer '96 collections, they discovered that she had morphed into a raven-haired temptress.

Nadja is an absolute professional: she enjoys a challenge, is punctual and assertive and takes her work very seriously. In a very short space of time she has conquered the modelling world.

And so the world now awaits the next move of this highly intelligent and industrious beauty. ©

UK AGENCY: **ELITE PREMIER**

NEW YORK AGENCY: **ELITE**

PARIS AGENCY: **ELITE**

NATIONALITY: **GERMAN**

HEIGHT: **5'10½"**

HAIR: **BLONDE**

EYES: **BLUE**

NAOMI
CAMPBELL

UK AGENCY:	**ELITE PREMIER**
NEW YORK AGENCY:	**WOMEN**
PARIS AGENCY:	**ELITE**
NATIONALITY:	**BRITISH**
HEIGHT:	**5'9½"**
HAIR:	**BROWN**
EYES:	**BROWN**

DARLING OF THE RUNWAY

Naomi Campbell is one of the world's true megamodels who, according to top designers such as Azzedine Alaïa, is also the Queen of the Catwalk. 'Naomi moves with a presence and magnetism that I have seldom ever encountered,' says Alaïa. Sassy, sexy and superfamous, the vintage model continues to reign supreme.

At the age of fifteen she was plucked from the streets of Covent Garden by Beth Boldt, a model agent from Elite with a famously discerning eye. 'She just glowed. I followed her to see how she moved, then walked up and asked her if she wanted to be a model. She said "yes", and that was it.' In 1980, Naomi was the first black model to appear on the cover of French *Vogue*. Cover shoots for British *Elle* and American *Vogue* followed swiftly. Then Steven Meisel photographed her and she immediately became part of the supermodel Trinity.

MODEL MOTHER

Naomi was born in 1970 in Streatham, South London. She was brought up by her stunning mother, Valerie, who, as an ex-model and dancer herself, has recently joined her daughter on the runway. With only nineteen years between them, Valerie and Naomi are more like friends or sisters than mother and daughter. Keen for her daughter to go into the performing arts, Valerie supported Naomi's career from the very beginning: sending her to dance school and then on to the highly regarded Italia Conti stage school. Before she had completed the course, Naomi was already establishing herself as an international model.

CELEBRITY

Naomi is a superstar. Not a month goes by when she is not in the newspapers, which are notorious for misinterpreting her no-nonsense attitude as that of a tantrum-throwing prima donna. She is a regular fixture in the gossip columns, which are filled with details of who she is alleged to be dating – past men have included boxer Mike Tyson, Robert De Niro and U2's Adam Clayton. When Naomi fell over on the catwalk in twelve-inch platforms, it made headline news.

BABY-WOMAN

When she is not sauntering down the runway this multi-talented star is working on her many other projects, including fundraising for such charities as War Child and Breast Cancer. She is author of the novel *Swan* – a story of five young models – and has recorded her first album, *Baby-Woman*. Naomi chose the name after a friend (designer Rifat Ozbek) had used these very words to describe her. More recent ventures include launching her very own Naomi doll and opening The Fashion Cafe with her supermodel buddies Elle Macpherson and Claudia Schiffer. Driven by extraordinary ambition, Naomi has become an accomplished actress. Her films include *Miami Rhapsody*, *Invasion of Privacy* and Spike Lee's *Girl Six*. She has also been a guest celebrity in episodes of *The Cosby Show* and *Absolutely Fabulous*.

Today, many black models have Naomi to thank for carving a niche in the marketplace. There have been many supermodels but Naomi, a veteran, is undoubtedly one of the greatest. ©

ELLE

THE WORLD'S
BIGGEST
SELLING
FASHION
MAGAZINE

MAY 1993.

£1.80

HOT DATES
SUPERMODELS
AND THEIR MEN

LOVE IN EXCESS
THE PASSIONS OF
MICHAEL HUTCHENCE

HOLIDAY FLINGS
WILD CONFESSIONS

**THE RAPE
OF A NATION**
BOSNIA'S SHAME,
SERBIA'S GUILT

CELLULITE
HOW TO
LOSE IT

BEAUTY
THE NEW
NAKED FACE

**SUMMER
LOOKS
BRILLIANT**

NIKI TAYLOR

UK AGENCY:	**IMG**
NEW YORK AGENCY:	**IMG**
PARIS AGENCY:	**IMG**
NATIONALITY:	**AMERICAN**
HEIGHT:	**5'11"**
HAIR:	**HONEY**
EYES:	**HAZEL**

COVER GIRL

As a child Niki Taylor always had a burning desire to become a model. At thirteen her dream became reality when she was accepted by an agency in Florida, and then went on to win a Fresh Faces contest run by a top New York model agency. Her prize was a $500,000 modelling contract.

Niki's first experience of modelling was dampened when, after returning from a shoot in New York, she and her father found their car had been broken into and all their belongings stolen. But this did not hinder Niki, who had just found out about her first break: a cover for *Seventeen* magazine.

Since then, her career has been an explosion of covers, including *Elle*, *Vogue*, *Mademoiselle* and *Glamour*, advertising campaigns and, more recently, runway shows. Her flawless complexion and perfect features have earned her important cosmetic campaigns – Niki became the youngest model to sign a major cosmetics contract, with L'Oréal, for Cover Girl cosmetics.

NIKI INC.

At sixteen Niki Taylor was a millionaire and president of her own company, Niki Inc. Although she was represented by IMG model agency, Niki and her family decided to set up her own management company to handle tax and legal matters. Niki's mother, Barbara, now runs the company. Apart from Niki Inc. and her model agency, she has a network of people representing and working for her, including a publicist, personal manager, accountant and lawyer.

HOME FRONT

Niki grew up by the Florida coast. Her love of the sea and marine life led her at one time to contemplate a career in marine biology. These days she is able to support marine preservation by donating money and lending a helping hand whenever her hectic schedule allows.

Nick (as she likes to be called) has always been a great family girl and spends much of her spare time with them. More recently, she has started her own family with husband, the footballer Matthew Martinez of the Miami Dolphins. Niki and Martin now have gorgeous twins – Hunter and Jake.

CAREER

'To the majority of people Niki is the archetypal blonde, healthy, all-American girl and has been called the new Cindy. She's not! She is the first Niki who is guaranteed to sell magazines and products and is a favourite cover girl of *Elle*,' says Tomo Delaney, British *Elle's* bookings editor. Even today, the fashion world cannot get enough of her. 'Niki has a strong enough face and personality which have helped her recently carry off good, strong editorials.' Her Amazonian beauty, coupled with her versatility and energy have made Niki one of the highest earners. She has produced her own calendar and attracted worldwide press coverage.

This superstar has not allowed modelling to interfere with her education. After graduating from high school she went on to study special effects for film and television, and continued to take singing lessons and dance classes. This young model, mother and student has barely left her teens but has already accomplished more than many people achieve in a lifetime. ©

RACHEL HUNTER

UK AGENCY:	**STORM**
NEW YORK AGENCY:	**FORD**
PARIS AGENCY:	**FORD**
NATIONALITY:	**NEW ZEALANDER**
HEIGHT:	**5'11"**
HAIR:	**BLONDE**
EYES:	**BLUE**

BEACH BEAUTY

When Rachel was born in Auckland in 1970, little did her parents know that some twenty years later she would become one of the most famous celebrities New Zealand has ever known. Until she was seventeen, when her aunt persuaded her to try modelling, Rachel's only ambition was to become a beach bum. But she followed her aunt's advice and travelled to New York, where she signed up with the Ford model agency.

FRESH-FACED

It was the mixture of her fresh-faced beauty and pale blue eyes that launched Rachel on the path to fame. She had barely unpacked when the bookings started flooding in. Soon she was adorning the covers of *Vogue, Elle, Harper's Bazaar, Mademoiselle* and the highly reputed *Sports Illustrated*. Then came a tremendous leap up the rungs of the modelling ladder: she landed a major contract with Cover Girl cosmetics. Rachel was to represent the make-up range and become a spokesperson for the company.

FAMILY

In 1990, Rachel married rock star Rod Stewart, after he proposed to her in a California park. Before long the couple had started a family with the birth of their baby daughter, Renée. Rachel's body soon bounced back into shape and she returned to modelling for a couple of years, before becoming pregnant with her second child, Liam. Today Rachel divides her time between her homes in Essex, England and Beverly Hills, USA. She also likes to travel to New Zealand to spend a few weeks every year with her mum. Rachel has a very demanding schedule but, as a devoted mother, she tries to limit her modelling assignments so that she can be with her children and not miss out on any precious moments.

FITNESS GURU

Although Rachel has no aspirations to be classified as the Jane Fonda type, she has become something of a fitness guru. At a very early stage in her career she appeared in a body building video for *Sports Illustrated*. After having her second child, Rachel made her own fitness video with her personal trainer, Todd Person. She has also starred in the exercise show *Body*, produced by VH-1.

FAME

Rachel is far more than just a supermodel: she is an internationally renowned personality. Back in her native New Zealand she is treated like royalty. When one magazine put her face on the cover it increased the issue sales by 10,000. A television documentary of her life, *Rachel Hunter – Cover Girl*, was also a great success. Supermodel, celebrity and supermum – Rachel has it all! ©

STEPHANIE

SEYMOUR

UK AGENCY: **IMG**
NEW YORK AGENCY: **IMG**
PARIS AGENCY: **IMG**

NATIONALITY: **AMERICAN**
HEIGHT: **5'11"**
HAIR: **LIGHT BROWN**
EYES: **BLUE-GREEN**

BY SANTE D'ORAZIO COURTESY VOGUE, THE CONDÉ NAST PUBLICATIONS, UK

PHOTOGENIC

By the age of sixteen, Stephanie had inspired the modelling establishment with her enigmatic beauty and one of the most desirable bodies the industry had ever seen. Glance through the pages of *Vogue, Elle, Cosmopolitan, Allure* and *Marie Claire* and you will see her incandescent beauty. Her powerful presence has been captured on film by some legendary photographers: Herb Ritts, Helmut Newton, Arthur Elgort and Irving Penn.

ILLUSIVE DREAM GIRL

Over the last decade, Stephanie Seymour has enjoyed stellar exposure. Her face and body have endorsed numerous products: she was featured in Diet Coke's *Illusive Dream Girl* commercial and, with vital statistics of 34-22-35, helped take the lingerie company Victoria's Secret to new heights of success.

HAPPY EVER AFTER

In 1990, she took temporary respite from modelling when she became pregnant with her first son, Dylan. Her comeback, several months after his birth, was welcomed with riotous applause. A few years later she had her second child, Peter.

Stephanie has endured blanket press coverage of her private life, being romantically linked to rock star Axl Rose, Hollywood heart-throb Warren Beatty and Elite's John Casablancas.

Today, Stephanie is happily married to Prince Charles' polo friend Peter Brant. The couple reside in Connecticut, USA, with her two sons. When they married in Paris in July 1995, the paparazzi were there in droves. It was a spectacular occasion. Stephanie was dressed in an exquisite gown designed for her by Azzedine Alaïa that, coupled with their VIP celebrity guest list, made it one of the most glittering supermodel events. ©

DREAM EMPORIUM

During an interview with the *New York Times*, photographic guru Richard Avedon singled out Stephanie as being the most interesting and powerful model he had ever photographed. With her more than perfect measurements and gaze that says 'look-but-don't-touch', this walking dream emporium has the looks most models would kill for.

BACKGROUND

Stephanie was born in San Diego in 1969. As a child she spent many hours learning how to relax and lose control in front of the camera while her mother, a keen amateur photographer, used her pretty daughter as her model.

By her teens, Stephanie Seymour had developed into a tall, beautiful, and far from camera-shy young woman. A career in modelling seemed a natural progression. Stephanie saw Elite's Model Look competition as the perfect springboard into the profession. She entered the Californian heat and, although she did not win, she finished as a finalist and was taken onto Elite's books.

WEBB

VERONICA

RIFAT
OZBEK
Cotton skirt (£1,020) and
bra top, just seen, (£248),
both by Rifat Ozbek.

UK AGENCY: **STORM**

NEW YORK AGENCY: **FORD**

PARIS AGENCY: **FORD**

NATIONALITY: **AMERICAN**

HEIGHT: **5'10½"**

HAIR: **BROWN**

EYES: **BROWN**

ARTISTIC

Born in 1965 in Detroit, USA, Veronica had a traditional and disciplined upbringing. Her parents, who worked in the armed forces, were devout Christians and not encouraging of Veronica's ambition (as a dedicated follower of fashion) to study art and fashion. Instead, the Webbs wanted their clever daughter to pursue an academic route. Nevertheless, Veronica chose to take up art, and at sixteen moved to New York to study the subject.

DISCOVERED

Whilst at college, to help support her studies, Veronica worked part-time in a downtown Soho boutique. This fashionable part of Manhattan was a district frequented by model industry people and it was not long before someone spotted her great potential. Indeed, within one afternoon alone, three people approached Veronica suggesting she should model. Keen to pursue her artistic career, Veronica was apprehensive about modelling but, after a certain amount of persuasion, agreed to sign up with a New York agency. She was an instant success, and within a short time was working with photographic maestro Bruce Weber.

PARIS

To further her career, Veronica moved to Paris, where she soon started working for top designers. Here, she built up a great rapport with Azzedine Alaïa and went on to become his muse. During her two-year stay in Paris, Veronica's trump card turned up when, in 1992, she became the first black model to sign a major cosmetics contract: Revlon had chosen her to represent their *Colourstyle* range for black skin.

MEDIA

When Veronica returned to New York, her career took on a new dimension as she hit the big screen. She made her debut appearance in Spike Lee's cult movie *Jungle Fever*, which was followed by a part in the highly acclaimed *Malcolm X*. Not content with being a model and actress, this professional all-rounder aimed towards fulfilling one of her main ambitions: to become a writer. She is now an accomplished writer and recently became editor-at-large for *Interview* magazine. She has also written articles for such publications as *Elle*, *The Paper*, *Details* and the *New York Times*.

EXTRACURRICULAR ACTIVITIES

One of the funkiest and most stylish of the superpack, Veronica is an avid shoe collector – especially of the Manolo Blahnik kind.

This cultured American with a zest for life enjoys rollerblading, dancing and socializing. She also devotes time to supporting good causes and has recently become involved in the Fight Breast Cancer with your Bare Hands campaign for Revlon. Veronica has met Bill Clinton and regularly attends meetings at the White House with the aim of having a new bill passed which will help cancer victims.

Meanwhile, Veronica has carved out a career in broadcasting by hosting her own chat shows. She is also a singer and has recorded a single with Prince called *Pussy Control*. Supermodel, writer, broadcaster, actress and singer – startling achievements for someone who has barely turned thirty. ©

AMBER VALETTA

It was the fusion of a fresh face and gamine looks that made the fashion world fall in love with Amber Valetta. A new feather-cut hairstyle propelled her into the seventies revival mode and prompted top lensman Patrick Demarchelier to book her for *Harper's Bazaar*. Amber soon charmed other leading photographers such as Steven Meisel and Bruce Weber, with her calm yet radiant beauty. Then came her star prize – a major fragrance contract for Calvin Klein's *Escape*. DKNY, Valentino, Armani, Gucci, Jil Sander and other valuable campaigns followed. Her adaptable face is every make-up artist's dream, transforming from a cool, classic beauty into a modern-day Twiggy. As the fashion wheels rotate, Amber embraces each trend by changing her hair and image to match the new mood, and continues to be a favourite among the fashion world. 'Amber is a great beauty with chameleon-like abilities to transform herself,' says Zoë Souter, *Vogue's* booking editor.

Amber grew up in Oklahoma, and it was there, when she was sixteen years old, that she was spotted by a model scout. During Amber's early days as a model she was selfconscious about her protruding ears, but this very flaw only drew more clients to her.

Imagine this scenario: two models of the opposite sex meet on a shoot, become friends and fall in love. Amber met her future spouse, Hervé Le Bihan, during a shoot in France for Calvin Klein. Both Amber and Herve were featured in the advertisements for Klein's fragrance *Escape*. They married, in true celebrity style, in New Orleans – Amber cloaked in an exquisite John Galliano dress, surrounded by an entourage of star-studded guests. ©

UK AGENCY:	**BOSS**
NEW YORK AGENCY:	**ELITE**
PARIS AGENCY:	**ELITE**
NATIONALITY:	**AMERICAN**
HEIGHT:	**5'9"**
HAIR:	**BROWN**
EYES:	**HAZEL**

BRANDI

Superbabe Brandi is only seventeen and already a supermodel. Not only is she ravishing, but with her Sicilian and Puerto Rican heritage and full bee-stung mouth, she is delectably exotic, with the kind of mixed-culture beauty that the camera loves.

The 5'10" teenager was discovered by a talent scout from the Karin model agency in 1993, whilst on a local shopping trip in a town in Florida, USA. Within a month, Karin's flew Brandi to Paris and launched her onto the modelling circuit. At only fifteen, a mere babe in supermodel terms, Brandi needed to be chaperoned to and from her castings and assignments, and also needed a tutor to help her catch up on any missed schooling.

Top designers were quick to recognize Brandi's potential and started to book her for their shows. But before she had a chance to set foot on the runway at Christian Dior, her debut catwalk appearance was stymied. The French government, clamping down on underage models, prohibited Brandi from taking part in the show. However, the following season (having turned sixteen) Brandi was right up there sharing the runways with the premier-league supermodels.

Other models were soon outshadowed as leading fashion houses snapped her up. Karl Lagerfeld hired her for Chanel, and Gianni Versace used her for his sizzling supermodel campaign. She also appeared in a Paco Rabane campaign and was used to represent Katherine Hamnett's catalogue line. Brandi's extensive and high-profile client list now reflects her growing status in the modelling world. ©

UK AGENCY:	**SELECT**
NEW YORK AGENCY:	**NEXT**
PARIS AGENCY:	**KARIN**
NATIONALITY:	**AMERICAN**
HEIGHT:	**5'10"**
HAIR:	**DARK BROWN**
EYES:	**DARK BROWN**

BRIDGET HALL

BY NIALL McINERNEY

Her ascent was exceptional. Fourteen-year-old Bridget made the transition from freckle-faced schoolgirl to supermodel in less than a year. While her friends were reading classics and learning algebra, Bridget was signing up with a top model agency in New York. A few months later her agent sent her to Paris, where, within a matter of weeks, she was working with most of the prime players in the modelling business.

The greatest photographers fell under her spell as Steven Meisel, Patrick Demarchelier and the rest of the snappers queued up to photograph her. Soon, her face was to set magazine covers ablaze, as *Vogue*, *Elle*, *Allure* and other heavyweights recognized her potential. Bridget's wholesome beauty and her sensuality reflect the qualities of today's younger breed of supermodel.

By 1995, Bridget was an international supermodel earning in excess of two million dollars a year. During her prodigious career, she has already landed some of modelling's choicest advertising campaigns. She was the sun-kissed seductress who starred in a major Ralph Lauren campaign and she has also appeared in ads for Chanel, French Connection, Max Factor, Christian Dior and Guess?.

Modelling has earned Bridget the security to do exactly what she wants in life. Aged eighteen, the world is her oyster.©

UK AGENCY:	**IMG**
NEW YORK AGENCY:	**IMG**
PARIS AGENCY:	**IMG**

NATIONALITY:	**AMERICAN**
HEIGHT:	**5'10"**
HAIR:	**GOLDEN BROWN**
EYES:	**HAZEL**

CAROLYNMURPHY

Carolyn Murphy was strolling down the sidewalks of Manhattan one steamy summer day when she was spotted by a talent scout from New York's Women model agency. Since then she has worked non-stop, shooting with big names like Arthur Elgort, Pamela Hanson, Neil Kirk and Mario Testino for the premier magazines.

Carolyn has changed her hair colour from brown to bright red and then to grey. Her changeable quality is becoming her trademark. 'Carolyn is like a latter-day Linda Evangelista; she has changed her hair colour and style with perfect regularity, always giving people in the industry something new to work with. She also has the most beautiful blue eyes I have ever seen. She's great!' exclaims Tomo Delaney, British *Elle's* bookings editor.

Her first casting led to her very first editorial job – a fashion shoot for *Allure*. In less than a couple of years, Carolyn has found herself in the fashion pages and on the covers of dozens of glossy magazines, including *Harper's Bazaar*, *Mademoiselle*, *Vogue* and *Elle*. She has also been featured in campaigns for Escada, Istante, Trussardi and Et Vous.

Carolyn hails from Fort Walton Beach, Florida, but today resides in New York's Greenwich Village. She is a lively, energetic girl with a lust for life, who enjoys rollerblading and hanging out with friends. Photographers have described her as 'a breath of fresh air', as she brings enthusiasm to every shoot. Her place in the modelling world is now firmly assured. ©

UK AGENCY:	**STORM**
NEW YORK AGENCY:	**WOMEN**

NATIONALITY:	**AMERICAN**
HEIGHT:	**5'9"**
HAIR:	**BROWN**
EYES:	**BLUE**

BY MONIC RICHARD/COURTESY ELLE QUÉBEC

ELLE QUÉBEC

AVRIL 1995 N° 68   3,50 $

Harcèlement sexuel
Avons-nous trop crié au loup?

L'après-Scoop de **Macha Grenon**

La pilule qui empêche de vieillir
À surveiller de près

Benoît Brière au cinéma
Un premier rôle «parlant»... et comment!

Une **Montréalaise** à Moscou
5 ans d'exil à flirter avec le danger

spécial **mode 9 à 5**
l'élégance pratique

marieclaire *Anteprima moda*

LEI E LUI:
AMORE, LAVORO,
SALUTE...
CHI "VINCE"?

SHOPPING
PELLE A TUTTO
COLORE

ARREDAMENTO
LA CASA
NEOECLETTICA

NUOVO
EROTISMO:
SESSO AL
TELEFONO

UK AGENCY:	**MODELS 1**
NEW YORK AGENCY:	**ELITE**
PARIS AGENCY:	**ELITE**
NATIONALITY:	**BRITISH**
HEIGHT:	**5'11"**
HAIR:	**BLONDE**
EYES:	**BLUE**

CECILIA
CHANCELLOR

An ethereal English rose beauty, with impeccably refined features, Cecilia Chancellor has captivated the modelling world for over a decade. Well bred and well read, the ex-public-school girl began her modelling career at the age of seventeen when, following the advice of a friend, Cecilia approached the agency Models 1 in London. The fashion world took an instant shine to her angelic face, gawky frame and unkempt long blonde hair. And it was these assets that catapulted Cecilia into the limelight during the seventies revival in the mid-eighties. At twenty-six, she may have been one of modelling's oldest and most established waifs, but still had the capacity to portray a childlike innocence.

This versatile model continues to flourish, regularly gracing the pages and covers of *Elle*, *Vogue*, *Harpers & Queen*, *Marie Claire* and other glossy magazines. Ralph Lauren, The Gap and Barney's are just a handful of the many retailers in whose advertisements Cecilia has made an appearance.

During her career, Cecilia has taken time out to study art and these days she spends much of her spare time painting. Daughter of the former editor of the *Independent* magazine, she has also followed in her father's journalistic footsteps by writing a collections report for British *Vogue*. Cecilia is keen to move into film and has been sifting through film scripts. It won't be long now before she creates a stir in Hollywood. ©

EMMA
BALFOUR

UK AGENCY:	**STORM**
NEW YORK AGENCY:	**WOMEN**
NATIONALITY:	**AUSTRALIAN**
HEIGHT:	**5'8"**
HAIR:	**BLONDE**
EYES:	**BLUE**

Emma Balfour made her debut into the world of modelling at the age of seventeen in Sydney, Australia.

Her first assignment was a shoot for a local hairdresser, and that was soon followed by an equally uninspiring magazine shoot. Emma felt she was going nowhere and headed for Europe where, in London, her destiny lay waiting. Here she was snapped up by top model agency Storm and immediately started doing the rounds of castings and 'go-sees'. Then one day she decided to have her long blonde hair cut into a seventies-style urchin look, a style that was to be imitated by models worldwide.

A shoot for Australian *Vogue* depicted her new look perfectly. With her thin frame and gamine looks she epitomized the new trend. Suddenly, she

HIGH RIS

THE COOL SNAP OF AUTUMN CHANGE HAS BEGUN TO WHISTLE ROUND HIGH RISES, WAITING ROOMS AND LOBBIES AS SUBURBAN STYLES MAKE A SHARP POINT. THIS SEASON THE REVIVED V-LINE NECK LEADS THE WAY, ENSURING A TASTE OF SIXTIES DRAMA. PHOTOGRAPHS BY FRANÇOIS ROTGER

was being hyped all over the world. *Vogue*, *Harpers & Queen*, *The Face*, *Sky*, *Esquire* and other premier magazine shoots were thrust her way. Then came the runway shows and a number of prestigious advertising campaigns for Hugo Boss, The Gap, Armani, Christian Dior, Calvin Klein and Russell & Bromley.

Although Emma has joined the supermodel brigade and can now command up to £10,000 a day, she remains unaffected by all the attention. And as an affirmation of her down-to-earth attitude, Emma's ambition is to make enough money to be able to live on a farm surrounded by horses. Today, she likes to spend time relaxing (and sometimes working) with her fashion photographer boyfriend, David Sims. When David shoots his number one model, the results are enigmatic and end up as favourites in both their books. ©

33

HALLYDAY

ESTELLE

BY ANDRÉ RAU/COURTESY ELLE FRANCE

Estelle Hallyday stumbled into modelling by accident when she was approached by a talent scout whilst walking along a Parisian boulevard. The scout, who was from one of the leading Paris agencies, instantly recognized Estelle's potential and tried hard to persuade her to consider modelling. Estelle was flattered, but not convinced she had what it takes to be a model. The sixteen-year-old continued her studies, aiming for a profession in accountancy.

It was not long before the glamour of modelling became an attractive alternative to textbooks and calculators. To the delight of the model agent who had spotted her, she marched through the agency's doors. Estelle went on to become France's leading supermodel, gracing the covers of *Harper's Bazaar*, *Mademoiselle*, *Glamour*, and many international editions of *Elle* and *Vogue*. Some of her major campaigns have included Christian Dior, Vichy and Thierry Mugler.

Estelle has demonstrated that she has other talents, which have led her to become a television presenter on *Canal +*. Here she hosts an upbeat contemporary fashion/travel show that is aired in France. Married to French rock star David Hallyday, she spends time in Paris and New York, although one of her favourite places is the Caribbean island of St Barts. Estelle and David now have a baby girl called Ilona. In addition to her broadcasting career, Estelle is pursuing a new career in acting. Whether it's modelling, media or movies, her life is a great success. ©

UK AGENCY: **SELECT**

PARIS AGENCY: **KARIN**

NATIONALITY: **FRENCH**

HEIGHT: **5'9"**

EYES: **BLUE**

HAIR: **BLONDE**

FREDERIQUE

VAN DER WAL

UK AGENCY: **ELITE PREMIER**

NEW YORK AGENCY: **ELITE**

PARIS AGENCY: **ELITE**

NATIONALITY: **DUTCH**

HEIGHT: **5'11"**

HAIR: **BLONDE**

EYES: **BLUE-GREEN**

Frederique was studying economics and languages in Holland when friends urged her to enter Elite's model contest. As she was heading towards a career in business, she needed a great deal of persuading. Eventually, she decided to enter just for fun, and to her amazement won first prize. She immediately put her studies on hold and flew to New York to begin her two-year contract with Elite.

Once in New York, serious things began to happen. She landed major editorial bookings for *Harper's Bazaar*, *Glamour*, *Vogue*, *Mademoiselle*, and was regularly courted by *Cosmopolitan*. She was also 'the face' behind many advertising campaigns, including Revlon's Most

PHOTO: FRANCESCO SCAVULLO COURTESY COSMOPOLITAN USA

Unforgettable Woman in the World. Renowned for her curvaceous physique, Frederique is also adored by the lingerie giant Victoria's Secret.

Through worldwide recognition, modelling has enabled Frederique to combine her looks with her business skills and market her name as a brand. She has created her own swimwear line and launched her own fragrance, *Frederique*. In addition, she has ventured into lingerie design and has also produced one of the most successful keep fit videos on the market.

When not modelling or developing business projects, Frederique finds time to relax with friends, visit art galleries and go to the movies. To maintain her lissom shape, Frederique windsurfs, climbs, sails and takes part in other sports. ©

HEATHER
STEWART-WHYTE

Heather's rise from a free-spirited purple-haired punk to an international supermodel was unique. It all began in the depths of the English countryside, where at seventeen she worked as a nanny. She grew up on a farm and had ambitions to move to London and travel the world. So when she noticed a magazine article featuring a top London agency, she immediately reached for the telephone.

Heather, clad in punk attire, arrived in London and made her way to the Elite model agency. Elite recognized her potential, re-groomed her, and sent her out on castings and 'go-sees'. Her first job, where she had to sit staring at a wall for thirteen hours, soon dispelled any glamorous notions. Heather went on to model for many glossy magazines, but remained unfulfilled. After a year, she decided to take a sabbatical and set off backpacking around the world.

It wasn't until Heather was twenty-one that she settled in Paris and reappeared on the modelling scene. Her smooth, olive complexion and exotic features (derived from her Indian ancestry) caught the eye of the bookers at Elite's Paris office. Her breakthrough was on the cards and manifested itself in the form of an eighteen-page fashion story for *Joyce* magazine. Heather's track record now includes impressive campaigns for Yves Saint Laurent, Gucci, Chloé, Christian Dior, Lancôme and Shiseido.

These days, Heather lives in Paris with tennis champion husband, Yannick Noah. She is a dedicated supermodel who loves her work: 'Modelling is a true education in communication, photography and fashion.' ©

UK AGENCY:	**ELITE PREMIER**
NEW YORK AGENCY:	**ELITE**
PARIS AGENCY:	**ELITE**
NATIONALITY:	**BRITISH**
HEIGHT:	**5'10½"**
HAIR:	**BROWN**
EYES:	**GREEN**

IRINA PANTAEVA

From the vast icy planes of Siberia to the pages of *Vogue*, the incredible journey of this Eskimo model has fascinated the world. Twenty-two year old Irina stands 6' tall with long raven hair and large dark eyes set against a pale complexion. The girl from a fashion-starved country, who had always longed to own a pair of jeans, is now the model for Levi's Silver Tab. She has also inspired photographer Irving Penn to shoot her for an Issey Miyake advertisement.

Irina was studying design in Vladivostok when she entered and won a Moscow beauty contest. The contest took her to the catwalks of Paris, where she provoked immediate attention from fashion's most influential names. But her modelling career came to an abrupt halt when she was refused a visa. Eventually, through sheer persistence, she was granted an American visa and moved to New York to continue her modelling career. Within the space of a year she had a full quota of magazine

editorials to her name, including *Harper's Bazaar*, *Vogue*, *Elle* and *Marie Claire*.

Today, Irina lives in New York with her Russian husband, photographer Roland Levin. Although they originally met at an art gallery in Moscow they lost touch when Roland moved to America. But fate reunited them when, two years later, Roland spotted Irina on the runway at the Anna Sui show in New York. When she has a spare moment, Irina makes the long haul back to Siberia to visit her parents. The buzz surrounding her rise continues, as more of the media hail her as the leading Asian supermodel. ©

UK AGENCY:	**SELECT**
NEW YORK AGENCY:	**FORD**
PARIS AGENCY:	**THE MARILYN AGENCY**
NATIONALITY:	**RUSSIAN**
HEIGHT:	**6'**
HAIR:	**BLACK**
EYES:	**DARK BROWN**

JENNY SHIMIZU

Discovered working as a mechanic in a Los Angeles motorbike shop, Jenny Shimizu is far from your conventional supermodel. Raised in Santa Maria, California, but of Japanese origin, her ambition had been to become a cowboy. Later, her aspirations changed when she developed a knack for all things mechanical. Jenny made the decision to drop out of college when she was offered a place in a repair trade school. After her apprenticeship, she joined the Harley-Davidson custom design shop in Los Angeles.

The last thing Jenny Shimizu had ever imagined she would be was a model, and she was shocked when a casting director spotted her in a night club and asked her to star in his video. Since then, this most unlikely supermodel has never looked back. Jenny has been having a wild time hanging out with her fellow models and stars like Madonna.

This androgynous model, who sports a tattoo and wears a ring in her navel, is the complete antithesis of the glamorous supermodel. Jenny has pounded down the runways for designers like Jean-Paul Gaultier and Gianni Versace, who love her for her uncontrived beauty and for her masculine appeal. She has been photographed for all the high profile magazines, including *Vogue*, *Elle*, *Allure* and *Harper's Bazaar*, and has appeared alongside Kate Moss in Calvin Klein's *cK one* campaign.

Whenever she yearns for normality, Jenny just gets out the tool kit and tinkers around with her latest bike or car. ©

NEW YORK AGENCY: **WOMEN**
PARIS AGENCY: **CITY**

NATIONALITY:
JAPANESE/AMERICAN
HEIGHT: **5'7"**
HAIR: **DARK BROWN**
EYES: **DARK BROWN**

KIRSTY HUME

The first Scottish model to make it to the superleague, Kirsty spent her childhood years gazing in awe at pictures of top models. Her very first experience of the catwalk was when she took part in a local modelling and grooming course. Her modelling credentials were assured when she joined a London agency and began modelling in London and Paris. She was doing what the industry term 'bread and butter work' – catalogues, brochures and minor magazine editorials – but was getting nowhere. Then one particular Paris agent took a shine to her, and before long clients were falling over themselves to book her.

The eminent photographer Patrick Demarchelier gave Kirsty her first big break by photographing her for the cover of *Harper's Bazaar*. Countless editorial bookings soon came her way.

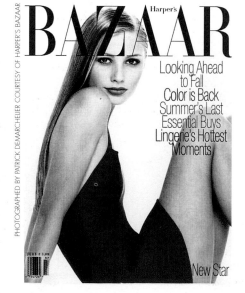

With her waist-length blonde mane and strong angular features, on the catwalk Kirsty turns into a shimmering superbeing. She has decked the runways of many top international designers, including Valentino, Gianni Versace, Guy Laroche and Giorgio Armani and has also attracted a coterie of big league advertisers, including Chanel, The Gap, Iceberg, Cerutti and Gucci.

Kirsty has settled in New York, but between modelling assignments she enjoys going home to her native Scotland to spend time with family and friends.

Her career may have been rather slow to start but has since gone from strength to strength and taken Kirsty right to the front line. ©

UK AGENCY: **ELITE**
NEW YORK AGENCY: **ELITE**
PARIS AGENCY: **VIVA**

NATIONALITY: **SCOTTISH**
HEIGHT: **5'11"**
HAIR: **BLONDE**
EYES: **BLUE**

KRISTEN MC MENAMY

BY NIALL McINERNEY

At eighteen, Kristen Mc Menamy was a quirky-looking teenager who could not find a partner to escort her to the senior prom. But what the boys did not know was, that in a couple of years her uncommonly beautiful face would mesmerize the fashion world.

From the start, modelling did not come easy for Kristen. Although she was lucky to be signed to a top agency, the prime bookings always seemed to go to another model. Eventually, she decided to take a drastic measure and so she shaved off her eyebrows – and as if by magic, the fashion world suddenly took notice. Kristen was off-beat, unconventional and above all, different from any other model on the circuit.

One shoot with supermodel svengali Steven Meisel, and a star was born. She was also a hit with top photographers such as Helmut Newton, Herb Ritts and Richard Avedon, and has become one of the most photographed contemporary faces. In the world of advertising, she has recently appeared in campaigns for Prada, Chanel and Donna Karan.

These days, Kristen sports a less radical look and portrays a more womanly, classic image. Kristen's great love of fashion combined with her natural movement have singled her out as one of today's great runway stars.

Originally from Pennsylvania, Kristen now resides in New York with her baby daughter, Lily. Although she continues to model and has enjoyed a phenomenal career, motherhood has become her ultimate joy. ©

NEW YORK AGENCY:	**FORD**
PARIS AGENCY:	**FORD**

NATIONALITY:	**AMERICAN**
HEIGHT:	**5'10"**
HAIR:	**RED**
EYES:	**BLUE**

NAVIA

BY CHRISTIAN WITKIN/SYGMA/COURTESY W MAGAZINE

HENRI BENDEL, New York
ANNA SUI's acetate and polyamide lamé jacket, $300, halter top, $200, and HotPants, $200

She is sexy. She is exotic. And she is one of the few Asian models to reach supermodel status. Navia, who appeared from nowhere straight onto the fashion scene, soon had everyone in the industry asking 'who's that girl?' Born in Vietnam, Navia spent most of her youth in New York, where her family owned a chain of electronics stores. After finishing high school, she moved to London to pursue an education in art at the highly acclaimed St Martin's College of Art. She was rummaging around the flea markets in London's fashionable Camden Town when a photographer spotted her and introduced her to a top London model agency.

One of her very first photo shoots was for French *Vogue*, with top photographer Juergen Teller. Pamela Hanson, Ellen von Unwerth and Peter Lindbergh soon followed suit. She has also revealed her modelling talent in the fashion stories of *Harper's Bazaar*, *Vogue*, *Elle*, *Glamour* and *W*. Such achievements led to Navia being picked by Pirelli as the first Asian model to appear in their limited edition calendar. This femme fatale can also be seen on the runways alongside the superstar models working for such designers as Chanel and Mark Jacobs.

Away from the demands of the modelling scene Navia resides in New York and enjoys backpacking, camping and rollerblading, and practises yoga to relax. The ultimate goal of this successful superbabe is to become a top photographer. ©

UK AGENCY:	**MODELS 1**
NEW YORK AGENCY:	**IRENE MARIE**
PARIS AGENCY:	**CITY**

NATIONALITY:	**VIETNAMESE/AMERICAN**
HEIGHT:	**5'8½"**
HAIR:	**BLACK**
EYES:	**BROWN**

ROSEMARY FERGUSON

It happened in fairy-tale style. Rosemary was chatting with a friend over a burger and fries in a London branch of McDonalds, when she was spotted by top photographer Corinne Day. 'She looked absolutely beautiful, but completely different, with a look that is against what all glamorous models stand for,' says Corinne, who took Rosemary's first pictures for *The Face*. After the magazine hit the bookstalls, everybody wanted to work with her. But Rosemary, who was only fifteen and working part-time in a local supermarket, turned down bookings rather than risk losing her job. Eventually she shunned the fashion world altogether to finish studying.

When Rosemary returned to modelling a year later, the waif look was in, and with her flower-child looks she encapsulated the new trend. Soon her face peered out from fashion bibles like *Elle* and French and British *Vogue*. Later, she won a major campaign for Yohji Yamamoto and advertisements for Dolce & Gabbana, Strenesse and Nina Ricci.

Her effortless beauty and innocence have become her selling points. These qualities, along with a reputation for being good-natured, have helped her become a favourite among editors and photographers alike. Bookings editor at British *Elle*, Tomo Delaney, describes her as 'brilliant'. 'What I love about Rosemary is that she is down-to-earth, and for someone who is successful, has remained totally unaffected. She is a really sweet girl and great fun to work with.' ©

UK AGENCY:	**ELITE PREMIER**
NEW YORK AGENCY:	**ELITE**
PARIS AGENCY:	**ELITE**
NATIONALITY:	**BRITISH**
HEIGHT:	**5'10"**
HAIR:	**BROWN**
EYES:	**BROWN**

SAFFRON ALDRIDGE

From the day she was born, Saffron, who was named after the spice, was destined for success. Daughter of the famous sixties artist Alan Aldridge, she is the eldest of eight children, one of whom is top fashion photographer Miles Aldridge. Saffron's first attempt at modelling was unsuccessful when, after approaching several London agencies, she was rejected. Then she walked into 2 Management, an agency that saw behind a gawky sixteen-year-old the makings of a great model.

Saffron blossomed into a divine creature. But it wasn't until three years later that she made the transition from being just another ordinary model into an up-and-coming supermodel. Top lensman Bruce Weber noted her beauty and booked her for a Ralph Lauren campaign. This prompted Ralph Lauren to sign Saffron to an exclusive three year contract. When her contract ended, her career took off. She appeared on the covers and in the pages of numerous magazines and was featured in advertisements for Selfridges, Pretty Polly, Harrods and Burberrys.

In 1993, Saffron gave birth to Milo, a beautiful boy who often travels on shoots with her. Within six weeks of having Milo, she was in the studio being photographed for *Elle*. These post-natal photographs were taken by her brother Miles and are some of her most treasured pictures. ©

UK AGENCY:	**2 MANAGEMENT**
NEW YORK AGENCY:	**PAULINE'S**
PARIS AGENCY:	**VIVA**
NATIONALITY:	**BRITISH**
HEIGHT:	**5'9½"**
HAIR:	**BROWN**
EYES:	**BLUE-GREEN**

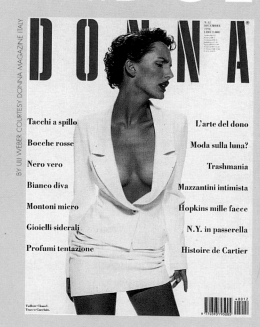

SHALOM

BY NIALL McINERNEY

Shalom is one of the most successful of the new generation of supermodels and has been hailed as the face of the future. She was born in Ontario, Canada, where she had a hippy upbringing – her name, very appropriately, means 'peace' in Hebrew. It was a stroke of luck when, aged eighteen, she was discovered by Canadian agent Anne Sutherland at a concert given by the rock group The Cure.

After working successfully in her native country, Shalom joined a top agency in the opportunistic modelling arena of New York City. First came the magazine editorials for *Vogue*, who were immediately impressed with her. 'Shalom is a modern beauty with great character and, since she has trained as a ballet dancer, she is incredibly elegant,' says Zoë Souter, British *Vogue's* bookings editor. Now her face shines out from the pages and covers of many international magazines.

The German fashion group Strenesse were one of the first advertisers to use her in a campaign that in the past had featured superstar models Nadja and Christy. Then came her major breakthrough. Karl Lagerfeld picked her for his 1995 Chanel brochure and for the Coco Chanel fragrance campaign. She has also appeared in ads for Jil Sander, Max Mara, Dolce & Gabbana and Gianni Versace. Shalom's ballet training has made her a favourite among designers such as Gianni Versace and Emanuel Ungaro, who hire this dainty 5'11" mannequin for their runway shows. ©

STELLATENNANT

BY MANUELA PAVESIE COURTESY VOGUE, CONDÉ NAST PUBLICATIONS, UK

Great good buys

Wearing a ring through her nose and harbouring an eccentric, modern look, Stella Tennant represents a new breed of model that the fashion world has been crying out for. She is undeniably chic, but with a twist that sets her apart from her supermodel sisters.

From the day a friend introduced her to Plum Sykes, a fashion writer at British *Vogue*, Stella's route to the top looked certain. 'She is naturally beautiful, but has the capacity to look very different,' says Plum. 'But her great success can also be attributed to her charismatic personality and intelligent outlook.' Plum recommended Stella to Steven Meisel, who photographed her for French *Vogue*. Soon, bookings for British *Elle*, British and Italian *Vogue* and an abundance of other editorial assignments poured in.

Raised in Scotland, one of the aristocratic Tennant family, Stella was a somewhat rebellious teenager. At twenty-one, she graduated from art college armed with a fine arts degree and the aspirations to become a famous sculptor. But this ambition has been put firmly on hold.

Stella's entry into the supermodel legion was confirmed when she was chosen by Versace to appear in one of his prestigious campaigns. Other boosts were the D & G and Missoni campaigns. In the three years since she burst forth on to the modelling scene, her career has blossomed. Stella clearly remains a novelty to the fashion world, and they never seem to tire of her strong, up-tempo look. ©

TATJANA PATITZ

Tatjana Patitz has staying power. While many of today's supermodels had their heads buried in school books, her life was an endless merry-go-round of fashion shoots and catwalk shows. And, in spite of a lengthy career that spans more than a decade, Tatjana remains right at the pinnacle of her profession.

From an awkward, scrawny teenager, Tatjana flourished into a dream machine, with a body that turned most models green with envy. Not prepared to leave her career to chance, she travelled to Paris to visit the top agencies. She signed up with Elite, and by the time she was eighteen, she was on the cover of *Vogue*. Throughout her many years as a model, Tatjana has appeared on the covers and fashion pages of numerous magazines including *Vogue, Elle* and *Marie Claire*. Tatjana was also one of the first models to appear in the famous Levi's commercials. It was her statuesque frame, mass of blonde wavy hair and almond-shaped blue eyes that made the fashion world stand up and take notice of this Germanic masterpiece.

In 1993, between modelling assignments, she made her debut acting role in the box office hit *Rising Sun*. Tatjana, who was working alongside Sean Connery, played the high-class mistress of a Japanese businessman.

She now resides in Los Angeles where she enjoys going to movies and spending time with friends, especially with Gabriel Hill, her male model boyfriend. ©

UK AGENCY: **ELITE PREMIER**

NEW YORK AGENCY: **ELITE**

PARIS AGENCY: **ELITE**

NATIONALITY: **GERMAN**

HEIGHT: **5'11"**

HAIR: **DARK BLONDE**

EYES: **BLUE**

TRISH GOFF

'She has a very modern face which is perfect for now. Trish is a superb model and I am convinced she will have the capacity to alter her look as soon as the trends change,' says French *Vogue*'s fashion editor, Marie Amelie Sauvé. With her wide-eyed gaze and her coltish appearance she exudes the sixties look and has been described as a modern day Shrimpton.

Trish was plucked from her modest home in Florida by a New York photographer's agent. She began modelling in Miami and then moved to New York, where she was taken onto the books of a top agency. Since then, this little Lolita has charmed the modelling world. Fame came to Trish when she inspired key supermodel lensman Steven Meisel to photograph her. Subsequently, she has worked with some of the world's greatest photographers, including Richard Avedon, Arthur Elgort, Pamela Hanson and Annie Leibowitz.

Trish boasts a large portfolio of fashion editorials and front covers of Italian, British and German *Vogue*. She has numerous campaigns to her credit: Byblos, Versace, Max Mara, Kenar and, more recently, a prestigious cosmetics campaign for Elizabeth Arden. Trish Goff looks set to become one of the most memorable faces of the nineties. ©

UK AGENCY: **ELITE PREMIER**

NEW YORK AGENCY: **ELITE**

PARIS AGENCY: **VIVA**

NATIONALITY: **AMERICAN**

HEIGHT: **5'9"**

HAIR: **BROWN**

EYES: **BROWN**

YASMEEN GHAURI

Yasmeen Ghauri owes her mysterious beauty to her Pakistani father and German mother. From an early age, Yasmeen's ambition was to become an artist, and she spent many of her childhood years sketching and painting. Then one day, during a trip to a nearby hairdresser, she met her destiny. One of the hairstylists had connections with a local model agency and suggested she pay them a visit. She took his advice and, clutching a couple of snapshots, headed for the agency. They were immediately taken with her enchanting beauty and signed her up on the spot.

She was one of the first Asian models to hit the international circuit and, against all odds, become a supermodel. Yet for Yasmeen, reaching supermodel standing seemed a natural progression. Adored by designers for her elegant ethnic beauty, she soon became a darling of the runway. These days, she promenades down virtually every international designer's catwalk. Yasmeen has posed for major photographers and is featured in such top fashion magazines as *Elle*, *Vogue* and *Harper's Bazaar*. Her principal campaigns include Revlon and Ralph Lauren.

Yasmeen spends her free time rollerblading, skiing and playing pool. She is also a championship backgammon player and avid cyclist. Today, most of her time is taken up by modelling, but in the future she hopes to be able to turn her childhood hobby into a profession and become an artist. ©

UK AGENCY: **SELECT**
NEW YORK AGENCY: **NEXT**
PARIS AGENCY: **THE MARILYN AGENCY**

NATIONALITY: **CANADIAN**
HEIGHT: **5'10"**
HAIR: **BROWN**
EYES: **BROWN**

YASMIN LE BON

British *Elle*'s very first cover girl – Yasmin Le Bon was the most famous British face of the eighties and has remained at the top of her field for twelve years, despite raising three children. In 1995 she was honoured when *Elle* invited her to co-edit their tenth anniversary edition. Daughter of an Iranian father and British mother, Yasmin Parvenah grew up in Oxford, England. She was introduced to her agency, Models 1, by a friend who was already on their books.

Yasmin, a classic beauty with an exotic twist, was soon working for high-fashion magazines and top photographers, including Peter Lindbergh, Arthur Elgort and Andrew Macpherson. Yasmin's booker (who has represented her for five years) believes the reason for her success and the longevity of her career is the fact that she is highly professional and never complains. 'Yasmin is the one who helps the assistant carry the boxes off the beach after a shoot,' says Karen Ford at Models 1.

At the age of twenty, Yasmin met her future husband Simon Le Bon, lead singer of pop group Duran Duran. A couple of years later, she gave birth to her first daughter Amber after working solidly throughout her pregnancy. Even at five months she could be seen treading the runways. Yasmin has since had two more children, Saffron and Tulula. Her children will always come first, but she successfully combines family life with the hectic schedule of a supermodel. ©

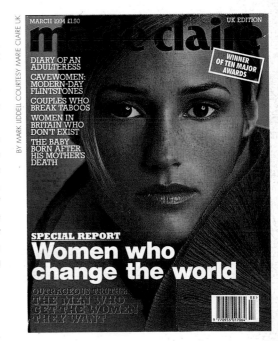

UK AGENCY: **MODELS 1**
NEW YORK AGENCY: **ELITE**
PARIS AGENCY: **ELITE**

NATIONALITY: **BRITISH**
HEIGHT: **5'9"**
HAIR: **DARK BROWN**
EYES: **BROWN**

MALE MODELLING

THE MALE SUPERMODEL

The media has at last turned its attention to the supermales: the new generation of male models who are well on their way to commanding the hype and earning power enjoyed by their female counterparts. Over the last decade the male model has made the transition from a mere accessory to the heights of a supermodel. And like the superleague females, supermales are launching calendars and fitness videos, and fast heading towards celebrity status.

MALE MODEL

The perception of male modelling as a profession has changed dramatically in recent years. Originally the field was seen as narcissistic: only for effeminate or vain men with inflated egos. These days, it is quite the contrary. Smart men know it is lucrative, and can act as a springboard to other exciting professions.

Modelling is one of the few industries where the earning power of women is higher than that of men. This is largely due to the size of the men's fashion and fragrance markets, which are considerably smaller than the women's.

Most male models start working in their teens, but often do not make the big time until they reach their mid to late twenties. Their female counterparts may command higher day rates, but male models have staying power. Their careers often continue well into their thirties, forties and, occasionally, fifties.

THE INDUSTRY

One of the major reasons for the expansion of the male modelling market was due to the growth in the 1980s of the men's clothing industry. Modern men were no longer content wearing a conservative dark grey suit to the office, and wanted an alternative to functional casual wear. Suddenly, in the age of conspicuous consumption, many of the major international womenswear designers were creating menswear collections; high street stores brought out more exciting ranges and basics for men, and designers launched diffusion labels aimed at the younger, more contemporary male.

Meanwhile, the number of men's fashion magazines multiplied as publishers were quick to supply the new image-conscious man. Simultaneously, style magazines were launched, aimed at the trendier, more off-beat guy. In addition, some of the top women's fashion magazines, such as *Elle* and *Cosmopolitan*, dedicated supplements or regular sections to men's fashion and grooming.

A spate of new agencies started to emerge, specializing in representing men. Established model agencies were also opening men's divisions to cater to this increased demand.

THE LOOK

The image of the male model has moved away from the stereotype hunk of the eighties and become more individual. The male is now portrayed in a vast number of ways: from a rugged and untamed rebel, or an offbeat, scrawny adolescent to a classically handsome, smooth dude. According to Brad Parson, the UK director of top international model agency Boss (with Marcus Schenkenberg and Gregg Spaulding among its models) the industry no longer wants only the archetypal chiselled square-jawed male. 'Clients want models with character who, although they may still be classified as good-looking, have a quirky, alternative look about them.'

Imagery depicting men as objects of desire has been adapted into men's advertising, with fragrance and fashion companies flaunting male sexuality in their provocative campaigns. In 1985, the first famous Levi's commercial featured model Nick Kamen in a launderette, stripping down to his boxer shorts. The advertisement was a huge success and inspired Levi's to produce many more unforgettable commercials featuring drop-dead gorgeous guys wearing little else but a pair of 501s and a seductive expression. In contrast to these Adonis-like males, some advertisers, such as Calvin Klein in his CK campaigns are adopting a more alternative approach by presenting unglamorous visions of men. Sexuality is implied in an understated way rather than obviously flaunted.

The new breed of male models may not be walking million-dollar industries, but they are snapping at the heels of their female counterparts. Here is just a small selection of the best.

MARCUS SCHENKENBERG

Marcus is the Swedish supermale whose muscular torso became famous before his face in the Calvin Klein advertisement. He was discovered on a beach in Italy and since then has shot to fame. His earning power is now on a par with some of the female supermodels. With his untamed shoulder-length hair and rugged looks, he oozes sexuality and projects a very masculine image. Marcus can be seen in a variety of poses in his own calendar.

CAMERON

Cameron grew up in England and inherited his good looks from his Iranian father and British mother. After appearing in a Levi's commercial, Cameron's rise was meteoric, and he became one of the world's most sought-after male models. He has also produced his own calendar and is heading towards a career in acting. When Cameron is not globe trotting, he spends time at his Los Angeles home with his wife and his daughter, Azusena.

Pin-up: supermale Marcus Schenkenberg, from his 1995 calendar, photographed by Marco Glaviano.

Waiting in the wings.

Love is: Cameron on the runway.

Offbeat: Keith Martin struts his stuff.

MARK VAN DER LOO

Amsterdam-born Mark Van Der Loo, now resident in Paris, is currently one of the highest-earning and most in-demand models in the world. He is the epitome of today's male model with his alternative, yet highly commercial look. Mark has appeared in major advertising campaigns for Calvin Klein, Valentino, Armani, Trussardi, Boss and DKNY. His gorgeous Scandinavian-style looks have earned him prestigious editorial coverage in men's magazines around the world.

LUCA

Unemployed and homeless, Luca was discovered selling *The Big Issue* on the streets of London by photographer David Sims. Since then, he has never looked back. His rags-to-riches story was splashed all over the papers and soon he was working for some of the biggest names in the business, including *The Face*, *L'Uomo Vogue*, Levi's and Calvin Klein. His quirky, contemporary image also prompted Bruce Weber to pick him for a Versace campaign.

KEITH MARTIN

Keith was born in London in 1970 and as a child model had a head start against his peers. His large mouth and scrawny body have characterized him as one of the more radical male icons. These off-beat looks landed him work with designers such as

Yohji Yamamoto, Dolce & Gabbana, Sisley and Katherine Hamnett. He has also become a regular fixture in *The Face*, *Sky* and other style magazines. In between stomping down international runways and posing for top snappers such as Steven Meisel, he likes to spend time with his wife and child.

CHRISTIAN WILLIAM

Christian was a farmer from Idaho when, at twenty-two, he was discovered by a talent scout. He has been featured in numerous advertising campaigns, including Karl Lagerfeld, Valentino, Brylcream, Gian Franco Ferre and Nicole Farhi . . . to name a few. Christian, who was married at nineteen, has a seven-year-old daughter, Kailie, and looks forward to the free moments he can spend with her.

GREGG SPAULDING

This 6'1" American with strong angular features was spotted whilst working as an extra on a film set. Now he regularly graces the covers of such magazines as *Arena Homme Plus*. Gregg Spaulding's impressive resumé also includes ad campaigns for Daniel Hechter, Montana and Krizia Uomo. Recently *Arena* magazine paid tribute to Gregg by nominating him one of the top five supermales.

Catwalk parade: Christian William elegantly strolls along the runway.

Backstage: all tied up and ready to go.

Moose strikes a pose.

KEITH MALLOS
At the age of twenty, a top photographer spotted the potential of this ultra-hip yet unconventionally handsome American from Los Angeles and gave him his first big break. Now he has worked alongside supermodel Amber Valetta in a prestigious campaign for Gucci, and with Stephanie Seymour in *Harper's Bazaar*.

NICK MOSS
Brother of Kate, Nick was introduced to modelling by his supermodel sister three years ago. Nick has strong features, piercing blue eyes and prominent bone structure. At 5'11", his forte is mainly advertising and editorial, although he does do the occasional show. Nick has appeared in many magazines including covers for *W* and *FHM*. He was also the Levi's model in a recent advertising campaign.

GEORGE CLEMENTS
Photographer Corinne Day discovered George at Tooting Lido in London and she was immediately struck by his strong, quirky looks. George is a hit with photographers for his gentle character and laid back attitude. His modern, gamine looks won him a Calvin Klein campaign and spreads in such magazines as *Vogue Homme* and *Arena*. Today, George is based in London, but spends much of his time in Paris.

GABRIEL HILL
Boyfriend of supermodel Tatjana Patitz, American model Gabriel Hill is becoming a name in his own right. This shaggy-haired stunner has been described as having chameleon-like qualities for his ability to transform from a cool, funky dude, into a sophisticated creature. He is a major advertising model and has campaigns for Calvin Klein, Mulberry and Jigsaw under his belt.

MOOSE
Born in England, but of Indian origin, Moose was discovered by his agent Annette of So Dam Tuff whilst walking down London's Kings Road. Today, he is one of the world's top catwalk models and has also had major editorial exposure in magazines such as *GQ*, and *Vogue Homme*. He also has a full quota of advertising campaigns to his credit, including Kenzo, YSL, George Rech and Armani.

LARRY SCOTT
Discovered by a photographer whilst selling jewellery in a San Francisco store, Larry is now a leading supermale. At 6'1", with razor-sharp bone structure, his unique good looks have earned him campaigns for Banana Republic, Valentino, Armani and an *Eden* fragrance advertisement. In addition, Larry has appeared in almost every fashion magazine and on two covers of the highly prestigious *Vogue Homme*.

RISING ★ STARS

There are thousands of models working successfully, but only a handful will ever reach supermodel status. Who – or what – is it that elevates the select few to the ranks of up-and-coming supermodels?

Until the media dispelled the mystique surrounding the supermodels' rise, it was assumed that models were plucked from obscurity and catapulted to stardom virtually overnight. However, most people are now aware that many of the industry's biggest names – Linda, Cindy, Kate and Naomi – were modelling for years before hitting the big time.

The normal career path for a model is to spend a year or so in the new faces division, gradually building up her book by testing, doing the rounds of 'go-sees', and working for teenage magazines. Then, if successful, she will graduate to the agency's main division and work for a couple of years before – if she is exceptional – getting a major breakthrough.

More recently however, the media's insatiable appetite for new faces has led to models making a much faster ascent to Planet Supermodel. Models with superstar quality no longer have to wait years for their big break, with some making the transition from new face to up-and-coming supermodel in less than a year.

Every once in a while there is a girl with that million-dollar face who is destined to become a supermodel. She will skip the normal procedure of months of 'tests' and 'go-sees' and often leap straight from the new faces division to the agency's main tier. This model must have that special quality, that Eileen Ford classifies as the 'X factor', or what *Vogue's* bookings editor, Zoë Souter, terms as 'the right components'. 'A potential star should have that extra something that makes her stand out from the crowd,' explains Zoë. 'And as well as outstanding assets, she must have good bone structure and a modern, individual look.' But, it takes far more than just a pretty face and the right accoutrements. Potential supermodels must be smart, stylish and absolutely determined to become a star. Level-headedness and the right attitude helps the models to ride the highs and not lose direction when the going gets tough.

Above, rising star Lonneke – a budding beauty at the tender age of seven.
Right, the snap of thirteen-year-old Samantha that convinced Select to sign her up.

Once an agency has discovered the star quality in a model, they will nurture and mould her into a valuable commodity. Unlike a normal model, who takes years to cultivate, a starlet will be expected to learn the ropes in as little time as a few months. She is sent to the top hair stylists, shown how to apply make-up and kitted out in the latest fashions. Meanwhile, her booker will make appointments for her to see the industry's key people.

At this stage, confidence-building is an important part of the learning process. A rising star will not have the chance to gain experience through dozens of tests shoots – her first or second shoot may well be for real. Having confidence will help her feel at ease and open up in front of the camera. 'We suggest that a girl studies the poses of models in fashion magazines,' says Millie, one of Elite's new faces bookers. To prepare a girl for her first runway show, she is often sent to a trainer or dance classes to help her acquire rhythm and master the supermodel strut. Her first show season is the most important few weeks of her career, as seated in the audience will be an array of fashion editors and top photographers, often on the lookout for new stars.

The next step for the model is to be picked by one of modelling's superpowers: the exclusive group of top photographers, designers and editors, who have the power to place a model firmly on the map. When a major photographer such as Steven Meisel or Bruce Weber gets excited about a new model, the effect snowballs. Soon everyone is asking 'who's that girl?'

When this happens, within just a few weeks a model can become the hottest new thing on the circuit; a daunting experience for a fifteen-year-old. This kind of instant success is rare, and usually only occurs in most agencies once every year. At this crucial stage, it is down to the skill of the booker to orchestrate the model's every move. They must be highly selective as to who the model works for, saving her for the prestigious glossy magazines and top advertising campaigns. The wrong kind of exposure could easily burn her out.

BY JOSE ARAGON

BY JUSTIN SMITH

*Polaroids from Jade Parfitt's first job, **left**, and Emma Blocksage's first test shoot, **below**.*

***Below**, Jodie Kidd's very first show season – seen here at the Calvin Klein show in New York.*

A rising star is hot property to her agency and it is in its interest to make sure she is well looked after. Agents will put the model up in their model apartments and provide a chaperone to accompany her on castings and assignments.

Looking after such a young stable of girls is not easy. It is the booker's job to inform them about the modelling profession, but it is difficult for a fifteen or sixteen year old to understand the prestige attached to certain elements of the business. Agents try to educate the model and her parents about the importance of working with top photographers and high-fashion magazines. Often young models would be happier working for the teenage publications and other magazines they can relate to. 'It is so easy for us to become wrapped up in the superficiality of the business, and forget that a young girl is naive to the internal snobbery,' admits Select's new faces booker, Sarah.

Very few young girls can handle the pace, competition or rejection, and it takes a girl with special qualities to succeed. She must have stamina and tenacity to be able to deal with the problems of travelling, being away from home, or missing a boyfriend. Agents are careful not to push the youngest starlets like fourteen-year-old Lonneke too hard until they are old enough to cope. Others, like Jade Parfitt, take time out to continue their education. But for the likes of Jodie Kidd – who shot to stardom almost overnight – the pressures are immense. Modelling may be very glamorous, but giving up your youth for a haphazard career is not easy. However, for the select few, like the models featured on the next few pages, the rewards will be well worth the sacrifice. ©

BY NIALL McINERNEY

JODIE KIDD

MOTHER AGENCY: SPIRIT MANAGEMENT
WORLDWIDE: IMG

NATIONALITY: BRITISH
HEIGHT: 6'1"
HAIR: BLONDE
EYES: BLUE

Jodie Kidd is Britain's brightest new star – an extraordinarily beautiful seventeen year old who has taken the modelling world by storm. At 6'1" tall, with implausibly long limbs, chiselled bone structure and an utterly modern face, she has a look that cast her straight into the superleague. Her rise was meteoric: in less than a year since her first photo shoot she is a supermodel on the brink of becoming a household name.

Jodie inherited her exquisite looks from her aristocratic family. She is the daughter of top show jumper and polo player Johnny Kidd and great-granddaughter of Lord Beaverbrook, the newspaper tycoon. A country girl who loved horses, Jodie boarded at St Michael's School for girls in Sussex, England and joined the cadets, ending up as Corporal Kidd. She also developed a keen interest in show-jumping and polo, and after a short time she became a junior show-jumping champion.

This true life fairytale began back in September 1994, when celebrity photographer Terry O'Neill spotted sixteen-year-old Jodie at the Barbados Ball in London. Struck by her beguiling beauty, he introduced her to IMG model agency, who signed her up worldwide.

The fashion world instantly seized upon Jodie and within a week she was booked for the prestigious fashion pages of the glossies. British *Vogue* was one of the first magazines to fall under her spell. 'She is very striking with an ethereal quality which makes you look twice . . . She has a very modern look and her face captures the current look which has the sixties "mod" feel to it,' remarks Zoë Souter, *Vogue*'s fashion bookings editor.

During her first show season, Jodie was thrown in at the deep end, never having set foot on a catwalk or worn a pair of stilettos in her life. However, she strutted her stuff for no less than twenty-eight designers, including Calvin Klein, Isaac Mizirahi and Ghost, and soon developed her very own walk – the superslouch.

The future is bright – Jodie poses for Tatler, just one of the many magazines that had predicted she would be the face of the future.

HERE'S LOOKING AT YOU, KID

The face of the future belongs to Jodie Kidd, English designers' darling. Here, she dresses for dinner at Castle Howard in the autumn's most luxurious evening wear and tailoring. Styled by Kate Reardon. Photographed by JR Duran.

This page, long silver one-sleeved satin dress, £695, at AMANDA WAKELEY, 80 Fulham Road, SW3. *Opposite page,* long sequinned dress, £3,890, at KRIZIA, 18 New Bond Street, W1. Black bag with diamanté clasp, £195, by Anya Hindmarch, 91 Walton Street, SW3.

BY JR DURAN COURTESY TATLER, THE CONDÉ NAST PUBLICATIONS, UK

Jodie skipped the usual rounds of tests, 'go-sees' and castings and was working every day. After only three months, she had a book that would make most models green with envy, with stunning covers and fashion pages from *Elle*, *Marie Claire*, *Harpers & Queen*, *Mademoiselle*, *Tatler* and British, German, Italian and American editions of *Vogue*. Then came the booking for fashion bible *Harper's Bazaar*, which further increased her worth as a model.

As the requests for Jodie flooded in, her agent, being highly selective, wanted to save her for the choicest assignments. She was already hot property editorially. Then, as advertisers, keen to tap into her success, saw her as the face to sell more products, lucrative campaigns were thrust her way. Her photograph was plastered over the side of buses for fashion retailer Monsoon, on billboards for *You* magazine, and she was signed up to become the model for the new fragrance *Africa*.

Tipped by the fashion press to become the supermodel of the decade, Jodie had reached the privileged position of having DJ boyfriend Joel Chin accompany her on trips and backstage at the shows.

For a girl who had been modelling for just over six months, her ascent had been super-fast. But during the Spring/Summer 1996 collections – her second season – her career escalated from an apprentice model to a famous name. Her first stop was Milan. Here, the photographers chanted her name as she stalked down the runway with magnetic presence. Backstage, she was hounded by every film crew, photographer and journalist in town. By the time Jodie had touched down in London, her name was splashed across every single newspaper in every imaginable capacity. Jodie the new supermodel. Jodie the Aristocrat. Jodie criticized for looking super-thin. Jodie in Dolce & Gabbana. Jodie, Jodie, Jodie . . . the press and public could not get enough of her.

Since she began modelling, Jodie had worked every day and had travelled to Mexico City, St Barts, Miami, New York, Los Angeles, Milan and Paris on trips. So as the New York shows drew to an end, her agent suggested she take a well-earned break. Jodie headed for her parents' Caribbean retreat. And as she lay on a sun-kissed Barbados beach sipping an ice-cold drink and wearing a content expression, Jodie knew that she had already become one of the success stories of the nineties. ©

RIFAT OZBEK
Padded chiffon jacket, £565, and high-waisted velvet skirt, to order; sheer tights (just seen), £3.65, Pretty Polly; satin shoes, £175, Gina

BY TROY WORD COURTESY MARIE CLAIRE UK

LONNEKE ★

MOTHER AGENCY: PAULINE'S, NEW YORK/PARIS

NATIONALITY: DUTCH
HEIGHT: 5'6"
HAIR: LIGHT BROWN
EYES: BLUE

From her little town of Eindhoven in Holland to the New York studios of Bruce Weber, Lonneke Engel's journey into modelling was astonishing. At fourteen, Lonneke can only be described as breathtakingly beautiful – with full, pouty rosebud lips, long brown hair and startlingly blue eyes.

Lonneke's childhood dream was to become a model. As a child she would stare longingly at pictures of models in glossy magazines, hoping that one day she would be like them. By the time she was twelve, this independent little girl decided to take matters into her own hands and looked up the names of local model agencies in the telephone directory. Afraid that she might come across as nervous, Lonneke sat down and wrote a script, then telephoned the first agency on her list and read out what she had prepared. The agency were impressed by her initiative and invited Lonneke in for an interview. She was taken onto their books as a child model and soon started getting work with local companies.

A year or so later, a representative from top international agency Pauline's was on a scouting trip visiting small Dutch agencies, when she was shown Lonneke's picture. She immediately arranged for Lonneke and her family to fly to Paris and meet Pauline. At first glance, Pauline was overwhelmed by the captivating beauty of such a young girl. But what really impressed her was Lonneke's enchanting personality.

The series of events that happened next is almost unheard of in the business. No sooner had Lonneke arrived home, when she was summoned to New York for her first booking. Pauline had convinced top photographer Bruce Weber to hire Lonneke on the strength of just two child modelling photos. Lonneke could not believe her luck – her very first assignment was a prestigious advertising campaign and she would be working with one of the most famous photographers in the world. The job was for Abercrombie and Fitch and earned Lonneke $5000 and instant recognition as a rising star. The success of Lonneke's first job was re-affirmed when Bruce Weber re-booked her for an eight-page shoot for Italian *Vogue*.

Whenever Lonneke visits her agency she brings little presents for Pauline. Pauline remembers how Lonneke was beside herself with excitement the first time she watched her unwrap little gifts of salt and pepper pots and a milk jug in the shape of a cow. 'She is the most delightful girl,' says Bradley, director of Pauline's. 'She is polite, intelligent and well behaved, with all the potential to make a superstar.'

Pauline has encouraged Lonneke to have as normal a life as possible and will not allow modelling to disrupt her studies. 'At such

Above, Lonneke's first advertising shoot, by famous photographer Bruce Weber.
Right, her first test shoot, taken in Holland by Guiba Guimaraes.

a young age, she has years ahead of her, and we will look forward to handling her full-time as soon as she finishes school,' says Bradley. Back in her home town of Eindhoven, Lonneke is just like any other teenager: she plays the piano and enjoys her favourite pastime – horse riding. So far, modelling has been everything she imagined it would be and more. 'Being able to dress up, have fun and get paid for it – what more could I ask for?' says a very sweet and beautiful little Dutch girl. ©

KIRSTY McDONALD

MOTHER AGENCY: STORM

NATIONALITY: BRITISH
HEIGHT: 6'
HAIR: RED
EYES: BLUE

Kirsty was on a school trip in London when she was approached by one of modelling's most renowned talent scouts – Storm's Sarah Doukas. Even though she is a 6' tall, flame-haired beauty, Kirsty did not think she had what it takes to make a model, and could not understand what all the fuss was about. Sarah Doukas handed Kirsty her card and suggested she call the agency to arrange an appointment. 'I was sceptical at first, as you hear so many stories of girls being approached by con merchants, who promise to make you the next big thing. I think I was more receptive as it was a woman who approached me,' recalls Kirsty. But Storm was not offering empty promises. With Sarah's highly trained eye, she knew that Kirsty had enormous potential. 'Her looks were a mixture of Pre-Raphaelite and Boadicea,' says Sarah. Storm invited Kirsty and her parents to the agency for an interview. That very same day she joined Storm's new faces division.

At the time, Kirsty was sixteen, and at a boarding school that only allowed her to model during holidays. This frustrated clients more than Kirsty: after working with this unusual beauty they all wanted more. Kirsty did not need her parents or head teacher to tell her modelling was an ephemeral vocation. She was intelligent, and not prepared to sacrifice her studies for an unpredictable career.

After completing her A-level exams, Kirsty moved to London and devoted her time to modelling. For her first season she was booked for shows in Milan and Paris and was treading the runways of some of the top designers' shows, including those of Jean Paul Gaultier, Issey Miyake and Hermés. By the time she had returned to London, Storm had placed her with top agencies in New York and Paris.

From then on it was non-stop. She did a ten-page fashion shoot with Walter Chin for Italian *Vogue*. This was followed swiftly by bookings for Australian *Vogue*, American *Elle*, *Marie Claire* and a prestigious Spanish campaign with Linda Evangelista for El Cortes Inglés. She had also recently appeared in an advertising campaign for Clairol. Kirsty received even more recognition when she was chosen to be featured in a national breakfast television production, which included a series of programmes following the life of a model.

Later that year, Kirsty was told she had a place at Brunel University to study drama. An ambition of Kirsty's is to act or be involved in film, and the idea of becoming a television presenter has also crossed her mind. Kirsty knows what direction she is heading in, and is prepared to work hard and not just leave it to chance.

Above, disco babe. Kirsty poses for Gilles Bensimon for American Elle. **Right,** serene beauty for Japanese Marie Claire.

'I know that after working in such a glamorous and exciting business I will want an equally challenging career to fall back on,' explains Kirsty. The initial success of her modelling career prompted her to postpone university for a year. The college agreed to keep her place firmly open.

Despite the hype and incredible buzz that surrounds her, Kirsty remains level headed. It is her direct approach and positive attitude that have helped her succeed as a model. In the course of just one week, Kirsty had arrived back from shooting the new Levi's campaign with Albert Watson in New York and hardly had a moment to go on castings and visit her agency, before flying off to Paris for yet another major assignment. Clearly, this up-and-coming supermodel is going to go very, very far. ©

オーガンジーのブラウス（参考商
品）／カルバン クライン

53

EMMA **BLOCKSAGE**

MOTHER AGENCY: ELITE PREMIER

NATIONALITY: BRITISH
HEIGHT: 5'10"
EYES: GREEN
HAIR: BLONDE

'I know that I am going to be rich and famous.' These are not the words of a precocious wannabe, but of a very determined young model. In the summer of 1995, schoolgirl Emma Blocksage was just another hopeful, now she is well on her way to achieving her goal. Since she was seven years old, Emma has yearned for the chance to model. She has always admired the supermodels: 'My idol is Claudia Schiffer,' says Emma. 'I would love to look like her.' Emma had waited somewhat impatiently until she reached her teens to approach her school careers advisor. And it was there that she heard about Elite Premier.

At fifteen, Emma has more than her fair share of assets. She is sassy – with the capacity to portray a powerful image. Atop her voluptuous body is a luminous head of platinum blonde hair which frames the porcelain face of this sublime beauty. 'From the very first moment she walked into our offices I knew she was special,' says Millie, Elite's new faces booker. 'It is not everyday that you see a girl with such amazing potential.' For Emma, who had just finished her GCSE exams, modelling was the perfect way to fill her summer holidays.

Emma is a budding star. She has skipped the usual work for young magazines and started right at the top. After testing with two well-known photographers, Emma went on her first 'go-see' with the top fashion photographer Corinne Day. Corinne booked Emma for a shoot with the high-profile Italian magazine *Donna*. A few days later, she was booked for her second editorial job, with *Details* magazine. While other new faces models at her agency were doing the tedious rounds of 'go-sees' and castings, Emma was sent on her first trip abroad. With Millie as her chaperone, she headed off to Paris to be photographed for a fashion story for *Details*.

Emma was coping extremely well with the busy schedule, but the attention she had received in just two weeks was mind-blowing. Millie suggested that a week off, back in her home town of Hastings, would give her time to catch her breath. But this respite was cut short when top photographer Juergen Teller booked her for Italian *Vogue*. Another career booster came in the shape of a spread for *ES* magazine, who hailed her as 'Next

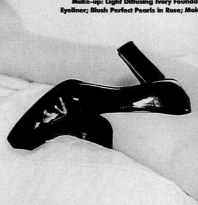

BY ALAN STRUTT FOR ES MAGAZINE

next y

She's blonde. She's beautiful.
babe to be exact, with Take T
Looks magazine in her backpack
from Hastings, is the 1995 Elite
compares pencil cases with her C
world and the Hastings schoolb
to supermodel Claudia Schiffer
on the

Cashmere sweater, £730; cashmere he
31 Sloane Street, SW1 (0171
Make-up: Light Diffusing Ivory Foundati
Eyeliner; Blush Perfect Pearls in Rose; Moist

Year's Supermodel'. Then, during her first season, she was the star of the Katherine Hamnett show and went on to illuminate the catwalks of many other international designers.

Meanwhile, Emma had entered Elite's national Model Look contest. She won first place. The following day Emma's picture adorned the front pages of the tabloids. Back at her agency, she leapt from the new faces division to join Elite Premier's main management tier. 'From the moment the word was out that Emma was the winner, everyone wanted to book her,' says her new booker, Sophie Wood.

A few weeks later, a rather apprehensive new model was off to Korea for the international final of the contest. 'I know there will be all these stunningly beautiful girls and I am convinced I won't win,' said Emma. But no sooner had she touched down in Korea, when word came back that the international press were going crazy over her.

In fact, she did not win, but came an extremely creditable fourth out of forty-seven contestants. In the eyes of the modelling world this is still a major achievement, and Emma Blocksage's name has already been added to tomorrow's list of superstars. ©

Superbabe fifteen year old Emma Blocksage is hailed as the Next Big Thing by ES magazine, photographed by Alan Strutt.

ear's model

a babe – a 15-year-old
her bedroom walls and
olgirl Emma Blocksage,
l of the Year. While she
choolfriends, the model
already comparing her
cking pictures of Emma
s – bedroom and office.

; and high-heeled loafers, £300; all Chanel,
nd 26 Old Bond Street, W1 (0171-493 5040).
hadow in Nightshade; Precision Brown/Black
ocolour in Nude Pink; all by No7, from Boots.

PHOTOGRAPH BY ALAN STRUTT

SAMANTHA ★
GODDEN-WOOD

MOTHER AGENCY: SELECT

NATIONALITY: BRITISH
HEIGHT: 5'6"
HAIR: STRAWBERRY BLONDE
EYES: AMBER

Samantha was a mere thirteen-year-old kid who read *Just Seventeen* and pinned Oasis posters to her bedroom wall. But her teenage world was turned upside down when her mother sent two snapshots of her daughter to London's Select model agency. 'I knew straight away from the pictures that she had great potential,' says her new faces booker, Sarah Leon. 'We invited Samantha and her mother to join us for an interview and immediately took her onto our books.' Samantha soon became one of Select's youngest new faces to gain international status. Before her fourteenth birthday she already had contracts with top international agencies in Paris and New York. Both agencies were desperate for Sam to arrive so they could comply with the requests of photographers. In New York, eminent photographers Ellen von Unwerth and Mario Sorento had seen her picture and were eager to meet her.

   She has been described as a child-woman. It is Samantha's angelic face, sultry look and mesmerizing amber-coloured eyes that convince top photographers to use her. Most new models usually test with at least three or four different photographers before being booked for a job. But Samantha's very first time in front of the camera was for real: a shoot with top photographer Juergen Teller for *The Face*'s main fashion story. This was followed shortly afterwards by a fashion shoot for *Vogue Homme*, photographed by Nick Knight.

   Meanwhile, Samantha's career was moving in two parallel lines. In between being photographed for the style press and prestigious glossies, she was working for young teenage magazines. 'This is very unusual,' explains Sarah. 'Most models leave the teenage publications behind at the first sign of a booking with a high-fashion magazine. But due to Samantha being so young, the photographers she has worked for respect this fact, and have not let the *Just Seventeen* covers and other similar work prejudice her career.' To Samantha, a cover shoot for *Just Seventeen* was far more important than appearing in *Vogue*. All her friends read *Just Seventeen*, and being on the cover has been the highlight of her career so far.

   Samantha is not your average fourteen year old. She appears shy, but knows exactly what she wants, and underneath the coy

Above, Samantha's favourite picture.
Right, Her first job, photographed by Juergen Teller for The Face magazine.

facade is a very confident, composed young person. The professionals agree that once she is in front of the camera she transforms, bringing energy and enthusiasm to a shoot. 'For such a young model, Samantha is most professional and obliging, and certainly seems to know the ropes,' says *Just Seventeen*'s fashion editor, Stephanie Stevens.

   Aside from modelling and attending school, Samantha pursues her main hobby – roller skating. It was her refreshing attitude to life that made her turn down the chance to work for Calvin Klein, because she did not want to miss out on a roller skating event with her friends. At only fourteen, Samantha Godden-Wood knows she has the world at her feet. ©

Velvet tailcoat by Richard Tyler from Browns; diamanté horns from Portobello Market, London W11

JADE PARFITT

MOTHER AGENCY: MODELS 1

NATIONALITY: BRITISH
HEIGHT: 6'
HAIR: BLONDE
EYES: BLUE

Jade Parfitt symbolizes the new-age model. At 6' tall, with a quirky, alternative look, she is definitely not your conventional model. But it is precisely this uncontrived beauty that has raised seventeen-year-old Jade to the status of future supermodel.

Her very first taste of modelling was when, unbeknown to Jade,

In questa pagina.
Lungo, diritto e sottile il
cappotto in panno
nero di Yohji Yamamoto,
a disegnare una
silhouette ieratica.
Scarpe Stephane Kélian.
Scala Autour du Monde.
Nella pagina accanto.
Revers contenuti e punto
vita appena accennato
per il cappotto doppiopetto
in panno di Giorgio
Armani. Moda Charlotte
Stockdale. Pettinature
Paul Lopez per Olga.
Trucco Lisa Eldridge per
Debbie Walters, Londra.

Above, understated chic – Jade poses for Italian fashion magazine Donna. *Right*, funky for British Elle.

her mother entered her into a television modelling competition with *This Morning*. At fifteen, the idea of modelling had never entered the mind of this country girl from the south of England, whose favourite pastime was riding horses. So it came as a great surprise to Jade when she won the contest and secured a prize contract with top London agency Models 1.

Incredibly, her very first show booking was for Prada in Milan. Jade's booker, Tori, escorted her and remembers watching nervously as this rather gangly teenager took her very first steps on the runway. 'She was a little bit stiff,' recalls Tori. 'But this was not surprising, considering she was the only unknown among the world's premier league supermodels.' Prada was the launching pad for Jade's career. The word was out. Steven Meisel, along with the rest of modelling's key players, wanted to use her. She was booked for the collections in Paris, including the Rifat Ozbek show, and that was followed by appearances in almost every New York show. Back at the agency, the phones rang non-stop. Jade was in demand.

Over the next few months, her career took off faster than that of any of the other new faces models Tori had worked with. 'It was phenomenal,' says Tori. 'I have been a booker for seven years and Jade's is one of the fastest ascents I have ever seen.' She landed the Calvin Klein jeans campaign, shot by Steven Meisel, and was booked for the prestigious fashion magazines such as *Harper's Bazaar*, Italian *Vogue* and *The Face*. Soon she was being represented by the Ford model agency in New York and Paris.

It is her professional and down-to-earth attitude that has helped Jade rise to the top. 'She is a star pupil,' says Tori. 'Jade has never thrown a tantrum and is always up front – she's a cool girl.' When Jade is in London she stays with Tori. 'It is just like having a friend to stay. She is the most together and mature seventeen year old I have ever met.'

Jade is as bright as she is beautiful. Straight As in her English, Drama and Media Studies A-level exams have proved that Jade is not prepared to let modelling jeopardize her chance for a place at university.

In two years, Jade has made great accomplishments in her modelling career and has become a star in her own country. She has received acres of publicity from newspapers and magazines who have been following her success story. In addition to her portfolio of prestigious tear sheets, Jade has worked for two of the fashion world's most important titles – British *Elle* and French *Vogue*. *Elle*'s bookings editor, Tomo Delaney, sums up the secret of her success: 'Jade has a slightly off-beat look and is a very different type of beauty. There is much more to girls like Jade than your conventional text book beauty.' ©

Suits and boots
The new tailoring is slick and streetwise.
Sharp satin. Skinfit leather. Velvet underground

MODEL AGENTS

The epicentre of Elite Premier's offices – the booking table.

They have been labelled the superagents: an exclusive handful of model agents who represent the top fashion models. The superagents control their models' destinies. Once an agent has signed up a new recruit, they will cultivate and build the model, carefully plotting every step of her career. And if she is lucky enough to reach the top, the agent must strive to keep her there. These exclusive model agencies are situated primarily in the world's fashion centres – Paris, New York and London.

Model agencies are fast becoming international corporations. Elite have the largest network, with twenty-five offices around the globe. IMG and Ford are two other powerful corporations who, along with high-profile agencies such as Company, Wilhelmina, Metropolitan, Pauline's and Boss, all have more than one base.

glossy magazines that adorn agencies' walls. But, as they are constantly jetting around the world, to see them in the flesh is a rarity. However, agencies act as a base for most of their models, and a regular stream of gorgeous creatures can usually be found decorating the offices. Some turn up to chat to bookers or update their books; others to attend the occasional agency-based casting. Agencies are also swamped with nervous wannabes, anxiously waiting to be seen, and to find out if they have the looks required to make a model. The bookers (the agency staff who handle the models) usually sit around a large circular table known as the booking table, which encompasses a rotating filing system containing charts – their models' schedules. From these tables, models will be booked for assignments all over the world.

INSIDE THE AGENCY

A model agency is the epicentre of the modelling business. Imagine the buzz of a city broker's trading floor; the commodity – beauty and youth. Supermodels can be recognized from the covers of

THE MOTHER AGENCY

When a model first starts out with a model agency, this particular agency becomes known as the model's mother agency. Even when a model is placed with foreign agencies, the mother agency

60

still retain overall control of the model, and take a cut of the commission the foreign agencies earn. Some models do make a habit of switching agencies; however, most stay loyal to their mother agency.

THE INTERNATIONAL BUSINESS

Since the globalization of the model industry, almost every fashion model works internationally and will often be signed to an agency in London, New York and Paris. The two primary modelling capitals are Paris and New York, with London, then Milan following close behind. Tokyo is another city where models can be found. It is a good market for models to earn bread-and-butter money and build up their books. New faces models are often sent to Tokyo or Osaka on six-month contracts. For model agents, the international market has opened up many doors. 'The business has gone great guns since it became global. It is so exciting now that we have the whole world to play with,' says Sarah Doukas, Storm's managing director.

To an outsider, the international network can appear complex. A model may be with Elite Premier in London, but this does not automatically mean she will be with Elite in Paris or New York. It often depends on who the model's mother agency is. Agencies like Storm, in London, who are one of the largest independents in the world, will work with most of the other top foreign agencies. 'Through being independent we have the advantage of being able to work with practically all the New York and Paris agencies, including the networks,' says Sarah Doukas. 'We work regularly with Women and Next in New York, as well as with Ford, Company and Wilhelmina. Although Elite and IMG have offices in London, this does not prevent us working with their foreign branches.'

Once the agencies have set up a working agreement, they follow a sort of trading system with their models. A London agency will place a top model with an agency they are affiliated with in New York, and will expect them to reciprocate by sending a model of a similar calibre.

A MODEL AGENT'S ROLE

The structure of an agency is divided into tiers: the new faces division, main model management and a top tier for the superstars. Each division is run by different bookers, often on separate tables. If the agency has a men's or mature models' division, they will also be handled separately. The general role of a model agent is to represent its models by managing and promoting them. But the duties extend much further than this.

The booker's role depends on the models they are representing. If they are handling new faces models, the job will involve everything from nurturing the model and hyping her within the industry, to sending her on 'go-sees' (industry jargon for appointments) with photographers and magazines. It is also down to the booker to mould the new recruits into perfectly groomed, polished models. They will arrange 'tests' and help build the model's book. Occasionally, if necessary, bookers will chaperone young models abroad.

Bookers who run the main division will often spend their day negotiating fees, booking assignments, sending models on castings, and organizing the models' foreign trips. They arrange everything from hotels to facials, manicures and personal trainers.

There are bookers who exclusively manage the premier tier – the supermodels. They will handle all the supermodels' special projects, such as videos or books, as well as their press interviews and television appearances. Supermodels are always in demand and invariably receive many more requests than they could ever possibly accept, with both the first and second 'options' always taken. Therefore, their bookers are in the unique position of being able to select who the model will and will not work for and spend most of their day turning work away. It is crucial that a supermodel only works for the high-fashion magazines and the most prestigious clients, especially new supermodels, for whom one wrong move could damage their reputation and cost them future bookings.

PUBLICISTS

Some superstar models, such as Cindy Crawford and Niki Taylor, have their own publicists in addition to their model agencies. These publicists do not handle bookings, but are hired to help regulate the model's media exposure. It is they who decide which television appearances and press interviews the model will accept.

SCOUTING

To fulfil the constant need for fresh faces, agencies must continually look for new models. Model agencies are inundated with letters and calls from aspiring models and spend considerable time assessing them. They also employ scouts to go out in search of new talent, although many models are discovered by chance. The scout's hunting ground can be anywhere from schools to shopping malls, in all corners of the world. Once found, the new discovery is taken under the agent's wing. Each one is a gamble, but every once in a while they will have discovered the next Kate Moss.

Elite Premier's new faces booker, Millie, admires one of her model's books.

MODELS' LIVES

Models appear to live life in the fast lane. They jet-set around the world, mix with famous celebrities and attend an endless stream of glitzy parties. But their lives are also physically gruelling: with demanding schedules, the stress of travel and fierce competition.

TOUGH AT THE TOP

Supermodels are the creators of dreams and have become the most aspired-to and hero-worshipped icons of the nineties. Under the constant glare of the spotlight, they are under immense pressure to keep a high profile, look glamorous, and be seen in all the right places, doing the things models are supposed to do. If they step out of line, their glossy image could be in jeopardy.

Models' lives can be extreme. From partying hard for weeks on end, to early nights and healthy regimes, they work extremely hard, with rarely a spare moment to themselves. It takes a level-headed, disciplined person to cope with such a demanding schedule. Jetting around the world may epitomize the high life, but soon loses its initial allure. Most models long for life's normalities: spending time in their homes, visiting their friends and family, shopping or simply going to the movies. Travel can put an enormous strain on models' relationships, as they often go weeks without seeing their partners, especially when they, too, have a demanding career.

Models are constantly surrounded by the most beautiful women in the world. And with such great emphasis attached to their looks, they are often pressurized into examining themselves too closely. Beauty is ephemeral, and all models are aware that there is always someone more beautiful or youthful just around the corner.

Becoming a supermodel may make you rich and famous and open the doors to every party in town, but sacrificing your freedom and anonymity is a stiff price to pay.

PUBLICITY

Most models move in the same social circles as other famous celebrities and often date or marry rock stars or Hollywood heart throbs. The double act becomes the choicest prey for the paparazzi, who pursue them twenty-four hours a day. Press exposure is inescapable for supermodels. As celebrities, they are expected to be seen in public, and only when they are behind closed doors can they retain their privacy. Some have become so famous that they are escorted around town by bodyguards.

Bad publicity has conjured up a gruesome image of an industry rife with drugs, anorexics and decadent young models who live off a diet of alcohol and cigarettes. Drug taking may have been prevalent in the sixties, seventies and even eighties, but today's models are far more likely to be seen around town with a bottle of mineral water. And as April Ducksbury, partner of top London agency Models 1 points out, 'Any youth industry, like the modelling or music business, is bound to be associated with drugs. But these days modelling is so highly competitive that most models would not dare risk doing anything that could affect their looks.'

The idea that models are all anorexic and rarely eat is a terrible misconception. Anorexia is a severe disorder that can a destroy model's appearance by leaving her gaunt-looking, with lined skin and hollow eyes. An anorexic model would never be able to work; she would not have the stamina, and even a top make-up artist would not be able to conceal the telltale signs. 'Most models are naturally thin and have hungry metabolisms. They eat plenty of the right foods and most do not need to diet,' insists April.

PERKS OF THE JOB

Modelling is glamorous and fun, and a great way of meeting interesting people. It also acts as a springboard to many other exciting careers. And for those who reach supermodel status the

Supermodel, supermum and superwife: Yasmin Le Bon, backstage at the shows with husband Simon and daughter Amber.

CASTINGS

GO-SEES

A MODEL'S **TOOLS**

BOOK

Models' books are their most important sales tools, comprising a selection of their best photographs and current tear sheets (pages torn out from magazines). In addition to their main books, supermodels have press books that include press cuttings of all their major magazine and newspaper interviews. Models always have at least one duplicate book at their agency. Whilst the model is on an assignment, the agency is busy sending the second and third book out to clients.

New faces models often start with only four or five test shots in their books, whereas a supermodel's book will contain a mixture of approximately fifteen of their strongest covers and tear sheets from high-fashion magazines. Many of the tears will be current, although the models and bookers have favourites that stay in the books for years. Models rarely include advertisements in their book, as these pictures are usually too commercial.

PHOTOGRAPHS BY PETER LINDBERGH FOR HARPER'S BAZAAR

Surreal: Hugh Grant elevates Linda Evangelista to great heights. A spread from Linda Evangelista's portfolio, from Harper's Bazaar and photographed by Peter Lindbergh, courtesy of her agency Elite Premier.

Karen Mulder's card, courtesy of her agency Elite Premier.

PHOTOGRAPH BY MICHEL THOMSON / COURTESY VOGUE FRANCE

KAREN MULDER

Height 5'10 . Dress 6 . Bust 33½ . Waist 23½ . Hips 34 . Shoes 8 . Hair Blond . Eyes Grey Blue
Hauteur 1.78 . Confection 36 . Poitrine 85 . Taille 60 . Hanches 86 . Chaussures 39 . Cheveux Blonds . Yeux Bleu Gris

COMPOSITE CARD

The composite card is usually an A5 printed card that features a selection of the model's strongest images, with details of the model's name, vital statistics, and agency. Supermodels usually put their most stunning magazine cover on the front, and favourite tear sheets on the back.

Cards vary depending on the model and agency, but in general show one or two head shots on the front and three or four full-length images on the reverse side. Some are printed as colour gatefolds, others are simply two-sided black-and-white cards. Models leave copies of their cards wherever they go. They act as a reminder to photographers, magazines, and clients, who will often file them for future reference.

EDITORIAL

Editorial refers to the cover, fashion and beauty pages of a magazine. High-fashion magazines (known in the industry as the fashion bibles or glossies) feature top designers' clothes and hire major photographers to shoot their covers and fashion stories. The pay for models appearing in them is low, but the work is extremely prestigious and gives the model the right kind of high-profile exposure. Models also gain by creating strong images for their books. Apart from the glossies, there are a host of other fashion magazines that act as a stepping-stone to these leading titles.

Vogue, Harper's Bazaar and *Elle* are the illustrious magazines synonymous with the supermodels. To appear on their covers is one of the highest accolades a model can receive. From then on the model's day rate increases dramatically, and they are in a position to command higher advertising and show fees.

Editorial fashion pages are also highly sought after. The model will be booked for a fashion story that is usually several pages long. The fashion story may feature one model exclusively in what is termed as an 'only girl' booking, or could include several models. Beauty editorial is not quite so desirable for the model due to the photographs often being printed small or surrounded by text. Occasionally however, when

magazines use full-page images, they can work well in a model's book. While models are building their books, they are often sent abroad to work for foreign magazines to get more tear sheets. Once the magazine has been published, the model can use the tear sheet in her book.

Right, a fashion tearsheet featuring Trish Goff.
Below, example of a beauty tearsheet – photo of Amber Valetta.

ADVERTISING

F

SHOWS

Each fashion season the supermodels travel to Milan, Paris, London and New York to take part in the collections. For models, the seasonal shows are the most demanding period of the fashion calendar spanning a week in each city for the ready-to-wear and slightly less for the designers' haute couture shows. Models may be booked for almost every show, flitting from one to another, with fittings in between. However, the hectic schedules of the superstar models only allow them to do a small selection of the big name designer shows in Paris, Milan and, to a lesser extent, New York. As most of the major British designers like Vivienne Westwood and John Galliano show in Paris, to spot Linda, Helena or their supermodel sisters on the London runways is a rarity. The big girls pick and choose who they parade for – Chanel, Versace, Prada, Gucci, John Galliano and Dolce & Gabbana are among their current favourites.

REHEARSING

Not every show needs rehearsing. Most of the models are so experienced that a brief run through, or verbal instructions of each scene's running order, will suffice. However, if a show entails complicated choreography, rehearsals are essential.

Each scene is carefully co-ordinated to ensure the model has enough time to change before her next parade. The second she steps off the catwalk, the model must make a frantic change into her next outfit, have her hair adjusted and make-up touched up, and regain her composure before her cue. The clothes are placed on a rail in running order so both the model and dresser know which outfit is next. Dressers are standing by to unzip, button-up and help the model with accessories.

THE SHOW BEGINS

The usual pre-show panic soon disappears as the show begins to run smoothly. After hours of preparation, each model will be on the catwalk for around ten minutes. Thirty minutes later, the performance is over. The models make a desperate dash to their next show.

Above, Nadja Auermann – only one minute to go. Centre, setting the scene – the backdrop of the Chanel catwalk. Right, showtime – Claudia Schiffer, Chanel's star muse, waltzes down the runway.

MAKE-UP AND HAIR

Models sit patiently in front of a mirror while the professionals transform them. The make-up and hairstyles will often follow a particular theme dependent on the season's trends and the designer's specific collection. Hair stylists and make-up artists, who also get their inspiration from sources such as movies, art and books, discuss the concept with the designers a few weeks before the show.

'A model's show make-up can take from half an hour to one minute,' explains top make-up artist Maggie Hunt. If a show consists of sixteen models, Maggie will make-up nine of them. The make-up is usually the same, slightly adapted to suit each model's individual features. 'The first model takes the longest. She is the example I follow when I set to work on the rest of the girls.' If the last show is running late, models do not arrive in time for the make-up artist to redo the make-up completely. 'When this happens I remain calm. In less than a minute, a few tiny changes to a model's make-up can make all the difference, with the colour and style reflecting the chosen theme.'

AT THE **ELITE MODEL** LOOK **CONTEST**

Cindy Crawford, Karen Mulder and Stephanie Seymour are just some of the supermodels who have entered the modelling profession through Elite's Model Look contest.

The setting is The Brewery, a smart venue in London's photographic district. It is Elite Premier's fourth Model Look competition: an evening that has already become known as one of the most glamorous events on the fashion calendar. The atmosphere is electric. Champagne is sipped by celebrities: Kylie Minogue, Bryan Adams and George Michael are among tonight's VIP guests.

A long table reserved for the judges lies empty except for the Disney character Goofy, who desperately tries to entertain the audience. There is an announcement over the Tannoy that the show will be starting in five minutes. A star-studded panel of judges slowly take their seats — designer Vivienne Westwood and singer Jason Donovan are among them.

Tension mounts backstage as twelve young wannabes, aged from fourteen to nineteen, prepare for what could be the most important fashion show of their lives. The twelve have been selected from thousands of entries. If they win, they will be taken on to Elite Premier's books, and are likely to become one of their future superstars. The winner will also represent the UK in the international final held in Seoul. The prize: fame, glory and a $150,000 contract with Elite worldwide.

The compères (two radio personalities) take to the stage and introduce the evening's star judge — supermodel Karen Mulder, ravishing in a long, white, sequinned dress. Meanwhile, the girls hover anxiously in the wings waiting for the music to start before they are unleashed onto the runway. It has been a long day, beginning with an appearance on the morning television show *The Big Breakfast*, followed by hours of hairstyling, make-up and rehearsals. Suddenly, the lights dim, music starts and the show begins.

The first contestant nervously struts down the runway wearing a micro mini and tiny tee-shirt. Kate, a 5'9" fifteen-year-old with fragile bone structure and tumbling chestnut curls, precedes blonde bombshell Pamela. The other ten follow. Some have duck feet, yet

others have managed to acquire the ubiquitous model swing. Each contestant must follow the same choreographed routine: down to the end of the runway and back, with the odd pivot thrown in, before disappearing behind the screen.

During the second scene the girls parade in cute china girl dresses and matching two pieces. These are followed by spectacular finale outfits: silver sequinned mini dresses accompanied by high, strappy sandals. The girls look great. By now they have gained more confidence — smiling and holding a longer pose to give the judges, press and television crews one last glance.

The show lasts about twenty minutes, and after a short break it is time to announce the winner. Two girls who tie for third place skip out onto the stage, followed by the runner-up. The audience yell and clap with delight as fifteen-year-old Emma Blocksage is announced as the winner. Supermodel Karen Mulder presents Emma with the winning sash and watches a rather shaky, but overjoyed new starlet head down the runway to success.

Opposite page, star-studded jury – Jason Donovan confers with another judge, while Lily Savage mulls over her decision. *Left*, girls, girls, girls – the contestants make their final parade. *Above*, crowned – the spotlight shines on the winner, fifteen-year-old Emma Blocksage.

SUPERHINTS

Supermodels epitomize the perfect woman. With the help of the professionals, models have mastered the art of making themselves beautiful. Here, the experts give tips on their tricks of the trade and supermodels reveal their health and beauty secrets:

Make-up artist to the supermodels **Mary Greenwell**'s key superhint is: 'Use as little base as possible, too much can mask the skin's natural tones. When buying foundation, always test the colour on your neck.'

Top make-up artist **Ruby Hammer** believes blending is the secret to great make-up. 'As professionals, we spend half of our time blending in the eye colour and blusher, then softening and chiselling until we get the perfect finished result.'

'A hair-cut without colour is like a face without make-up,' says international hairdresser **Terence Renatti**. 'Most models colour their hair. It not only enhances their appearance but adds volume.'

Supermodel **Veronica Webb**'s attitude to exercise is to take up something you enjoy. To keep in great shape, she runs once a day and enjoys rollerblading.

'Neat, well-shaped eyebrows make all the difference to your face. Pluck them from underneath the arch, or go to a professional,' advises **Emma Bannister**, *Marie Claire*'s beauty editor.

Top make-up artist **Charlie Duffy** suggests always covering eyelids with foundation and powder before applying eyeshadow.

For a beautiful complexion, supermodel **Stella Tennant** washes her face every morning with glycerine and rose water.

Supermodel **Jodie Kidd**'s beauty tip is to drink plenty of water and get lots of sleep.

Supermodel **Elle Macpherson**'s number one tip is to drink up to three litres of water each day.

To keep in shape, supermodel **Niki Taylor** eats healthily and works out regularly with a trainer, but does admit to having the occasional burger and fries, or her mum's lasagne.

Superstylist **Sam McKnight** says 'I believe people should make far more use of their hairdressers, who are usually more than willing to give advice on different styles and ways to wear your hair.'

'Nothing is more attractive than healthy-looking hair. To keep hair looking fabulous, my motto is: cut, condition and protect,' says leading hairdresser to supermodels and celebrities **Nicky Clarke**.

Top hairstylist **Colin Gold**'s tip for volume is: 'Apply setting lotion to roots or crown, place a couple of rollers close to the base of your head and leave in for a few minutes. If you still require more volume, slightly backcomb.'

To acquire the body of a supermodel, **Rob Lander**, personal trainer to the supermodels, suggests exercising with total concentration four times a week. 'Don't cheat on exercises – focus on obtaining your goals.'

'For an instant boost to make-up use a light ivory eyeshadow. It can be used to highlight your cheek bones or brow bone and can even be used to highlight your lips by putting a touch just above the cupid's bow,' says top make-up artist **Maggie Hunt**.

To stay fit and healthy supermodel **Karen Mulder** takes homeopathic supplements including magnesium, goldenseal root and echinacea.

SUPERHINTS

Opposite, Cindy – the prototype woman. **Left**, Christy – the flawless face of a classic beauty. **Above**, putting on the glitz.

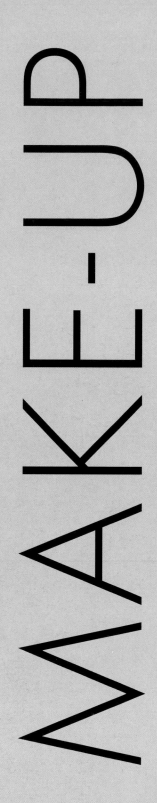

MAKE-UP

Mary Greenwell adds the final touches to Naomi's make-up.

Supermodels are fortunate to have learned the tricks of the trade from top make-up artists, and throughout their careers have tried and tested dozens of make-up combinations.

MAKE-UP ARTISTS

Mary Greenwell, Thibault Vabre, Maggie Hunt, Ruby Hammer, Dick Page and Topolino are some of the world's top make-up artists who can transform a bare face into a work of art. A model's face is like an artist's canvas, allowing the make-up artist to use a variety of colours and choices of application. Make-up artists make up models for fashion shows, magazine and advertising shoots. Show make-up is the most dramatic and artistically challenging. Make-up artists search for inspiration to be able to create anything from Egyptian eyes, tattoos, futuristic faces or a 1940s movie star theme – all with theatrical effect.

TRENDS

From the bare-faced natural look to luscious red lips or dark smouldering sixties-style eyes, make-up, like fashion, follows trends. According to make-up artist Ruby Hammer, people pay too much attention to trends, which often results in a look that does little to flatter their features. 'If you want an up-to-the-minute look, adapt the trends to your own face shape and features, and to what you feel confident with,' advises Ruby.

SUPERMODELS' MAKE-UP

Most supermodels stick to a look that really enhances their features, adapting it slightly to the current trends. Even supermodels have imperfections and need to accentuate their good points and disguise the bad. To acquire that supermodel look, learn natural, evening and party make-up from the top supermodel make-up artists, and spend time experimenting.

NATURAL MAKE-UP

Mary Greenwell advises how to achieve the perfect natural look:

BASE Wear very little or no base at all, using a dab of powder where needed. In summer, let skin breathe by wearing no base and just a little concealer where necessary.

EYES Apply neutral colours like browns, taupes and beiges to your eyelids. Avoid using eyeliner, although if you feel too bare without it, use a soft brown pencil around the outside corners of the eyes. Finally, use a dark brown or black mascara.

EYEBROWS Should be left as natural as possible. If you do feel the need to define eyebrows, use a soft grey eyebrow pencil with a browny undertone.

LIPS Choose a shade that matches your own lip colour, or alternatively opt for one shade darker. Terracotta and beige toned lipsticks are also good for a natural effect. Before buying lipstick, test it on the inside tips of your fingers. Disregard your lip pencil and apply the lip colour with a brush.

If you want to take your natural look one step further, or to avoid looking too neutral, apply a vivid red lipstick.

EVENING MAKE-UP

Maggie Hunt suggests how to create a stunning evening look:

BASE Start by applying a light-coloured cream foundation with a sponge, followed by a dusting of loose powder.

EYES Apply ivory matt eyeshadow over the whole of your eye area, from eyebrows to eyelashes. Using a small brush, apply dark brown or grey eyeshadow over and just above the eyelid, blending it out towards the corner of the eye. Use a soft black kohl pencil to emphasize the outer corner, smudging it from outer eyelashes towards the eyebrow. Also apply a line along the inside edge of the eye. To define eyebrows use a brown cake eyeliner.

CHEEKS Evening make-up requires a lot more colour than normal. Apply a rosy rather than bronze blusher on the cheekbones, instead of below them.

LIPS Begin by outlining the lips with a deep red-coloured lip pencil. Finally, use a deep red matt lipstick. This will last longer than any glossy or greasier type of lipstick.

PARTY MAKE-UP

A few changes turn Maggie Hunt's evening make-up into a special party look. After applying base and ivory eyeshadow as per evening look, use a semi-matt brown eyeshadow along the eye contour and under the bottom lashes. Next, apply a black cake eyeliner above top lashes and a brown cake liner to eyebrows.

FALSE EYELASHES 'Trim a third off the edge, then, without applying any glue, rest them on your own eyelashes to see if they suit your eye shape. Next, apply a thin layer of glue. Let them dry completely, then apply a second layer and put them as close to your own lashes as possible. Finally, shape them to match your own, and apply a thin layer of mascara.'

To complete this look, use bronzing powder instead of blusher. Finally, for lips, use a fleshy brown lip pencil to outline, followed by a very pale Bardot-like lipstick.

TOOLS OF THE TRADE

A make-up artist's kit is a treasure trove of colourful palettes, as well as the following make-up basics: make-up sponge, eyelash curler, velour powder puff, sable brushes, false eyelashes; base (foundation and tinted moisturizer; compact or translucent powder); mascara, eyeliner (cake, pencil and liquid); bronzing powder and blusher.

Below, Karen Mulder goes for gloss.

Left, Trish Goff in sixties-inspired make-up – nude lips, dark rimmed eyes and false eyelashes.

Dynamic duo – Linda with accomplice Julian D'Ys, the superstylist responsible for the chameleon's famous crop.

Straight and sleek, bleached, tousled, streaked or worn with a bang – top models are constantly changing their hairstyles. Some only tinker with their manes, but others fearlessly opt for dramatic new styles. A model is making a statement with her hair – it is about attitude, not wearability.

THE HAIR CREATORS

It is the creative talents of the session hairstylists that are responsible for the metamorphosis of the supermodels' hair. The world's top hairstylists – Julian D'Ys, Sam McKnight, Guido Palau, Colin Gold, Orlando and Oribe – are more than just stylists, they are artists. Julian D'Ys was responsible for Linda's original haircut and for Nadja's change to platinum. From their spectacular creations for the runway shows to their teased coiffures for photographic sessions, hairstylists work with models during the seasonal shows, as well as on advertising and editorial shoots. Each season requires new inspiration and a new theme. 'We are constantly thinking not only of the look for the moment, but for next season's look,' says top hair guru Sam McKnight.

TREND-WISE

Fashion trends extend to hair. When grunge was all the rage, models sported a messy, untamed look on the runway; the seventies revival inspired wispy feather cuts; forties retro put curls and waves back into fashion, which was followed by an explosion of bangs (fringes). The sixties influence witnessed models going two-tone and returning to big hair by revamping the bouffant and the Shrimpton-style bob . . . and so it goes on.

THE CHANGE

A change of hairstyle is the most effective way of altering a model's image and can evoke instant attention from the modelling world. Nadja Auermann was propelled to stardom when she bleached her hair a ravishing blonde. Linda Evangelista is another supermodel whose career took off when she cut her long hair short. After Helena Christensen adopted blonde streaks in her dark brown hair, many other models were seen wearing the accentuated streak, or blonde block at the front of their hair. Amber Valetta and Emma Balfour also took a turn in the right direction when they had their long hair cut into the gamine look.

CROWNING GLORY

For models like Cindy, Claudia, Karen and Carla, their long tresses are as important to their image as the latest cut is to their shorter-haired pals. Such models will alter the style very slightly and occasionally change the colour, but will never lose one of their most precious commodities. Models with long hair usually wear it tapered around the front or, if it is very sleek, cut in a blunt line. Models never perm their hair. Not only is it bad for its condition, but it prevents them wearing it in a variety of ways. Long hair can be very versatile: it can be worn up in a top knot or pony tail; backcombed or curled; or simply adorned with hair slides. For an instant change, wigs and hair pieces are also favoured by models and hairstylists.

Models with shorter hair have the advantage of being able to experiment with many more styles and colours, and alter their identity more radically. Linda Evangelista is the colour queen, changing her hair colour almost every season. Short hair can also be more easily adapted to suit the current trends by layering, shaping, or simply styling in a different way.

Beautiful and well-groomed hair should be *de rigeur* according to the superstylists, including Sam McKnight, whose personal philosophy is the 'five-minute hair' – so that your hair should take no longer than a few minutes to style. 'The vast range of products available make today's hairstyles quick and easy to achieve at home,' says McKnight.

HAIR CARE

Models' hair is teased, back-combed and covered in gunge almost every day – inevitably resulting in dry, damaged hair. With the emphasis on glossy, healthy locks, good hair care is essential. Frequent use of heated appliances, too much sun or chemical changes such as colouring, can also damage the hair. The condition of the hair can be helped by using the right products, such as gentle shampoos, intensive conditioners and regular treatments, that feed the hair, leaving it smooth and silky. Most models have a deep conditioning treatment at least once a week. A good, balanced diet, along with vitamins such as cod liver oil, C, E and B-complex will nourish the hair from its roots. And finally, to keep hair in tip-top condition, leading hairdresser Terence Renati recommends a six-weekly trim.

Right, superstylist Sam McKnight, who has his own product range, adds a hair piece to Helena's hair. **Below**, Oribe, hair maestro and owner of an ultra-hip New York salon, tousles Niki Taylor's mane.

Supermodels may be naturally beautiful, but their looks are their fortunes, and most maintain disciplined beauty rituals to keep them looking good.

There are the exceptional few who claim they never exercise and can eat what they like, but most models take their beauty regimes to extremes, employing their own dermatologists, aromatherapists, personal trainers, beauticians and nutritionists.

There are several elements that contribute towards looking good: a healthy diet; a good skin-care routine; plenty of sleep; regular exercise and fresh air. For a holistic approach it is important to combine all these factors and, as *Marie Claire's* beauty editor points out, have fun while you are doing so. 'Look after yourself if it makes you feel good,' advises Emma Bannister. 'Enjoy experimenting with new beauty routines, rather than seeing it as a chore.' To look good, follow the basic supermodel beauty guide:

SKIN CARE

Models must have flawless complexions, so it is essential that they follow a good skin-care routine. The key to impeccable skin is not just expensive products, but making the time and effort to look after it.

CLEANSING Skin should be cleansed with a cleansing lotion or cream, facial wash or cleansing bar, but not soap. To remove make-up, a cleansing lotion or cream is preferable.

TONING A toner should gently remove any traces of make-up and help close the pores. It also helps to moisten the face in preparation for the moisturizer. Avoid toners with alcohol, as they strip the skin of its moisture and natural pH balance. An effective natural toner is a mixture of witch hazel and rose water.

MOISTURIZING It is important to keep the skin well moisturized. Dry skin may require richer creams, whereas a pH-balanced lotion is more suitable for oily skins. To promote cell growth and boost the circulation, spend a couple of minutes each day massaging the moisturizer into your skin.

EXFOLIATING This is a way of removing dead cells and dry skin from the skin's outer surface. The most effective exfoliation is a facial scrub. To boost circulation and allow skin to breathe, it should be used once a week. Those with delicate and sensitive skins should avoid using abrasive types. Natural ground oatmeal is a gentle, yet effective way of exfoliating.

SPOTS AND BLEMISHES Even models get the odd spot or skin blemish that can be disguised by using concealer, or by turning the spot into a Cindy Crawford style mole. But, as most models would agree, the best advice for a clear skin is to eat a healthy, well-balanced diet, and get plenty of sleep. More severe skin problems such as acne, can be treated effectively with homeopathic or other natural remedies. For severe acne, doctors can treat sufferers with antibiotics, the contraceptive pill or Retin A gel.

FACIALS Regular facials can improve the texture of the skin and give it a healthy glow. The deep cleansing process also helps reduce spots and blemishes. There are many types of facials available; all achieve a similar result.

SUN CARE A tan may look great, but it causes irreparable long-term damage to the skin. In very small doses it can stimulate vitamin D production, which creates a feeling of well-being. Use fake tan to achieve a bronzed effect that will look natural and will not cause any harm to the skin.

THE BODY

EXERCISE Models regularly exercise, to keep their bodies in peak condition. According to model fitness trainer Rob Lander, ninety per cent of supermodels have a personal trainer. 'The body is like a machine, it does not function correctly with the wrong fuel. How can you expect to look like Karen Mulder if you smoke, drink excessively and eat junk food?' says Rob. Exercising not only improves your physique, but has beneficial effects on your skin, as well as reducing stress and tiredness. Exercise of some form should be taken three or four times a week.

POSTURE To acquire poise and good posture, models used to walk with books balanced on top of their heads. Good posture helps to project a self-confident image, as well as improving the body's circulation. Dance and body conditioning techniques such as Pilates or The Alexander Technique all aid good posture.

AROMATHERAPY Today's models prefer alternative therapies like aromatherapy and homeopathy to relieve minor ailments such as stress, jet lag, headaches and colds. There are many essential oils with different healing properties available. Essential oils can also be used as beauty treatments for the skin and hair, but should always be diluted with a carrier oil, such as almond oil.

NUTRITION

The attitude to good nutrition should be about healthy eating and not drastic dieting. A good, balanced diet is the key to clear skin, shiny hair and a healthy body. Avoid refined and processed foods and try to eat five portions of fruit and vegetables and drink at least six glasses of water each day.

Opposite, fit for life.

FASHION

One trend – dictated by designers and expressed by models – captures the limelight each season. Fashion, however, comes in many guises and away from the spotlight an abundance of looks run simultaneously, complementing and contradicting each other.

THE LOOK

As the fashion pendulum swings, the model industry must redefine its perception of beauty to accommodate fashion's latest trends. Most models are versatile and able to re-invent themselves with the shifts of fashion. Linda Evangelista is the prime example of a chameleon-like model who refashions her image almost every season. Many other supermodels – including Kate Moss, Kristen Mc Menamy, Amber Valetta, Nadja Auermann and Stella Tennant – have recently adapted their looks to reflect the mood of the moment.

A few models, like Kate Moss and Emma Balfour, are overnight successes as they personify a current trend. Some of these models make money and disappear at the first sign of a backlash, but others, like both Kate (who became more womanly) and Emma, slip into a new trend with the greatest of ease. Then, there are the lucky few who are classically beautiful, possessing, like Christy Turlington, Karen Mulder and Claudia Schiffer, a timeless beauty that will continue to be in demand irrespective of the dictates of fashion.

In addition to having a certain look, models are expected to generate different moods both on the runway and in front of the camera. A model may be required to look vampish, voluptuous, sexy, sultry, androgynous, angelic, innocent, childlike or play the part of the *femme fatale*, boyish imp, fresh-faced country girl, girl-next-door, diva or temptress at the click of the camera's shutter.

THE TRENDS

The first look to stem from the supermodel era was the glittering image that typified power dressing and the superficiality of the eighties. Glamour was the buzz word – with impossibly glossy models squeezing perfectly proportioned bodies into impossibly glitzy outfits.

Then came a backlash that was the very antithesis of eighties' fashion – grunge. This anti-fashion movement inadvertently gave birth to one of fashion's most memorable looks. To represent it, the fashion world required a scrawny wisp of a model with a childlike innocence and untamed hair. She came in the shape of the waif. Kate Moss was the first to epitomize this look, but other waifs, such as Emma Balfour and Tania Court, soon followed. Rosemary Ferguson and Cecilia Chancellor were two other waif-like models who encapsulated the seventies revival craze with their hippy chick, flower child looks.

A new radical look was formed as a band of quirky and androgynous models were seen stomping down the runway. Headed by Kristen Mc Menamy with shaven eyebrows, Stella Tennant sporting a nose ring and tattooed Jenny Shimizu, this band were not only hired to represent directional designers' way-out techno-gear or new-age punk designs, but became favourites among even the most conventional designers. Nadja Auermann and Eva Herzigova brought new glamour to the runways, with their luminous white hair and sublime

New Glamour, Eva Herzigova

Waif-like, Cecilia Chancellor

Androgynous, Kristen Mc Menamy

beauty. And with their coltish, Shrimpton-esque looks, Trish Goff and Jodie Kidd typified the sixties 'mod' revival.

SUPERMODEL STYLE

For some models dressing with style is intuitive. Others have gleaned it from fashion editors and designers. But one thing is certain, models have a distinctive sense of style. Supermodels possess some of the latest designs; it is a perk of the job. They then skilfully team their designer labels with classical pieces or funky little numbers from high-street stores, to create their own individual image.

Helena Christensen is an example of a model with strong personal style. 'She has excellent taste and natural flair for mixing and matching clothes,' says French *Vogue's* fashion editor, Marie Amelie. Models like Helena also favour second-hand designer shops or flea markets for special one-off vintage pieces to add to their wardrobes.

'Some of the supermodels I work with turn up in jeans and a T-shirt, others always look extremely chic. However, irrespective of what they are wearing, they nearly all carry a black nylon Prada bag,' explains Lucy Sykes, fashion assistant editor

Ethnic grunge, Kate Moss

of *Harper's Bazaar*. Along with the ubiquitous Prada bag, models favour other fashion items such as Chanel jackets, Prada's or Gucci's minimalist dresses and separates and Calvin Klein's basics in a theme of black and white or neutrals, occasionally punctuated with vivid colour. For parties many adore Azzedine Alaïa's body-hugging numbers and John Galliano's creations.

Models spend most of their lives having to look glamorous, so when they are relaxing or travelling, they dress down. They wear practical, understated basics such as jogging pants, T-shirts, Levi 501s, simple dresses and tunics.

CASTING CLOTHES

The dress code for castings is simple: clothes that flatter and show off the models' assets. Micro minis and tiny tops are worn with platforms, chunky heels or Converse-style trainers. For the winter casting look, add a pair of tights and knee-length boots, and throw a warm coat or jacket over the top. Alternate with black pants, Levi's, skinny ribs and white shirts.

Sixties remixed, Trish Goff

THE FASHION CYCLE

Five decades of fashion items, looks and icons that, as fashion evolves, continue to be recycled and revamped for the catwalk:

1950s

- rock'n'roll
- teddy boys
- pencil skirts
- Chanel couture
- bikers
- rockabillies
- bandannas
- capri pants
- drainpipes
- crombies

1960s

- hippies
- kaftans
- Mary Quant
- the mini
- psychedelia
- Biba
- Vidal Sassoon
- Mods
- rude boys
- PVC
- A-line skirts
- cheesecloth
- skinny-rib jumpers
- zip-up knee-high boots
- head scarves
- space age
- hipsters

1970s

- preppies
- the maxi
- skinheads
- punk
- Malcolm McLaren
- Vivienne Westwood
- big hair
- Saturday night fever
- disco
- sequin boob tubes
- platforms
- boiler suits

1980s

- power dressing
- shoulder pads
- new romantics
- casual sweats
- designer jeans
- ripped 501s
- street style
- imitation Chanel
- the body
- lycra
- casuals
- goths
- trainers
- fake fur
- leggings
- indie kids

1990s

- grunge
- hippy revival
- seventies
- micro-mini
- technos
- acid
- glamour
- cyberpunks
- anything black
- forties dresses
- slip dress
- kimonos
- tiny T-shirts
- sixties mod revival
- satin
- space age
- jellies
- Versace couture

THE
COLLECTIONS

Supermodels, bright lights and pounding music set the scene for the
fashion designers' twice-yearly shows, known in the industry as
'The Collections'.

The front rows are reserved for the VIP fashion press – Vogue, Elle, Harper's Bazaar et al.

The collections are held in Milan, Paris, London and New York and are by invitation only – strictly for the VIP fashion press and fashion buyers – although the odd celebrity guest is welcomed. These exclusive shows take place in March and October. Designers always work six months in advance, so in October they will be showing their Spring/Summer ready-to-wear collection and in March their Autumn/Winter designs. Designers show their haute couture and menswear collections in January and July of each year.

These fashion extravaganzas have become far more than just trade shows. They are spectacular theatrical events. In 1995, film director Robert Altman attempted to capture the experience of The Collections in his movie *Prêt-à-Porter*.

VENUES

The shows usually take place in a large arena or in a tent that has been erected specially for the event. Occasionally, designers choose to show their latest collection in unusual or obscure places, such as museums, underground train stations or derelict swimming pools. More recently, designers such as John Galliano have abandoned the catwalk in favour of stage sets, where models strut across the floor in a cabaret-style production.

THE PEOPLE

Anyone who is a mover or shaker in the business is there, from the fashion director of Vogue and head buyer of Barney's to the royal guest of honour. The usual fashion industry greetings of 'air kisses' and 'darlings' can be found in abundance.

Seats are reserved for the fashion glitterati. A programme or brochure, sometimes accompanied by a gift, can be found on their chairs. Often the hosts have seduced their guests with freebies well before the show has begun. Gifts are sent to VIPs' hotel rooms or offices, in the hope that they will write good reviews of the show in their publications.

Catwalk photographers fight to reserve a good place close to the runway, to get the best angle on each outfit and, more importantly, each supermodel – Claudia Schiffer in the latest Chanel suit or Linda wearing a new skimpy Versace number. Some of their shots will fill the newspapers; others will appear in the catwalk sections and supplements of glossy magazines.

Above: the tents and purpose-built arenas lie empty as more and more designers stage their shows in unusual venues. Here, Issey Miyake goes Underground for one of his menswear shows, swapping the catwalk for a platform. Left: catwalk cabaret – John Galliano presents his collection on stage

81

THE CLOTHES

Many of the clothes featured on the catwalk are never really show pieces, often far too wild and outrageous for mass production. Their aim is to create a stir and attract maximum publicity. The Spring/Summer 1994 collections provided a perfect example of this, from designers Vivienne Westwood and Helen Storey, featuring models displaying bare bottoms. Not surprisingly these garments did not reach the stores.

BACKSTAGE

It is fashionable to keep everyone waiting: the longer the wait, the better the show. While the audience are often let get past security and take their seats for a long uncomfortable wait, behind the backstage is a hive of activity. The girls arrive in pecking order. The new ones first – often three hours before the show begins – and the veterans last.

Backstage is a happening place where the supermodels are not always on their best behaviour. It is chaotic and sometimes stressful, but it is also a great time for models to chat to each other and catch up on the latest industry gossip.

Top catwalk photographer Niall McInerney can be found behind the scenes at every show, observing the mayhem and capturing the backstage antics on film. It is organized chaos, comments Niall. Among the photographers, boyfriends and film crews is a team of highly skilled people who make it all happen.

While Kate is having her hair set in rollers, a make-up artist is applying a shimmering eyeshadow to highlight Amber's eyes. Pandemonium is going on around them as models arrive late from the previous show. I have seen models arrive only minutes before the show begins, leaving very little time for a change of hair or make-up, says Niall. For the privileged few who are allowed backstage, this extraordinary sight can be as entertaining as the show itself. It is a bit of a fabulous fantasy, sums up Niall.

PARTY PARTY

When the shows are over the partying begins, with a whirl of glamorous soirees thrown by the designers, magazines and, more recently, the supermodels themselves. Anyone who is part of the fashion scene will be partying until the early hours of the morning.

As the week of shows and parties draws to an end, the circus of press, models and their entourages prepares to take over the next fashion capital on the season's agenda.

Above, strictly for the catwalk.
Left, backstage mayhem – Kate Moss among the photographers, film crew, plastic cops, make-up brushes, lipsticks and rails of clothes. Opposite: main picture, ice maiden – Karen Mulder. Top to bottom... go for gold – Linda Evangelista; dramatic in red – Stella Tennant; happy chick – Naomi Campbell; East meets West – Kate Moss.

82

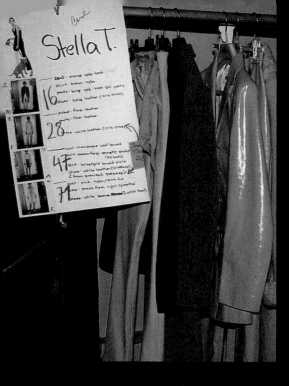

Running order.

Not just a pretty face!

The closest thing to Les Folies Bergères: one of Vivienne Westwood's muses.

Claudia grabs a bite before the show begins.

Supermodel pals Shalom, Amber and Kate sharing precious moments backstage.

A dresser helps Nadja make a quick change before her next parade.

Air-kissing originated here.

Even backstage, the bookings for Linda are still pouring in.

The partying continues backstage.

A good performance never goes unrewarded for Kristen.

FASHION
PHOTOGRAPHERS

Fashion photographers are some of the industry's prime model makers. In the past they discovered the models, today they give them their big break.

Linda Evangelista with Steven Meisel – a magic exists between a photographer and his subject.

SVENGALI

A select handful of the world's top photographers have the power to propel a girl to supermodel stardom virtually overnight by photographing her for the cover of *Vogue*, or picking her for a highly-prized advertising campaign. Steven Meisel, a suave New Yorker, is one of the most influential model makers, who took Naomi, Christy and Linda and turned them into The Trinity and Stella Tennant into a supermodel. Meisel works primarily for *Vogue* and for high-profile advertising clients such as Versace. He was also responsible for photographing Madonna's controversial book *Sex*.

Patrick Demarchelier, favourite photographer of the Princess of Wales and top lensman for *Harper's Bazaar*, is another one of modelling's kingpins whose Midas touch transformed Kate, Amber and Kirsty into supergirls. He recently launched his book *Patrick Demarchelier: The Photographs*, a collection of strong images, including shots of Stephanie Seymour, Naomi Campbell and other supermodels. Bruce Weber and Ellen von Unwerth, along with Peter Lindbergh, who sent Linda's career into orbit after photographing her original crop, are some of photography's leading Svengalis.

FEMALE PHOTOGRAPHERS

Until recently, fashion photography was a profession which was dominated by men. Today, however, a small group of top female photographers have created a major impact on the world of fashion photography. Pamela Hanson is a leading female photographer who rose to fame in the eighties with her black and white location shots. Pamela treats each session as if she were shooting a movie, capturing natural expression and movement from her models. Ellen von Unwerth, formerly a model, is one of the most famous photographers of today. Her imagery is striking, usually in black and white, and characterized with a strong identity reminiscent of film stills. She depicts glamorous and often heavily made-up females in spontaneous and provocative poses.

The most recent addition to the female elite is Corinne Day, who gets her inspiration from real people, and presents models in an understated, unglamorous way. With the world's most famous waifs as her subjects, Corinne's controversial approach to fashion photography has influenced the grunge movement.

Annie Leibovitz is one of the world's most famous celebrity photographers, who has also photographed many supermodels, including Cindy Crawford and Trish Goff. She started off her career working for *Rolling Stone* magazine and since then has photographed just about every famous celebrity, including Sharon Stone, Demi Moore and Arnold Schwarzenegger.

A RETROSPECTIVE

Fashion photography did not emerge as a serious profession until 1913, when photographer Gayne De Meyer was hired by Condé Nast to take experimental fashion pictures for *Vogue*. Fashion magazines of this ilk had before only employed illustrators to interpret the designers' latest creations. These authentic fashion images heralded the birth of fashion photography and De Meyer was firmly established as its pioneer.

Cecil Beaton and Edward Steichen took some of the earliest

Yasmin Le Bon, seen here enjoying a drink with David Bailey.

fashion photographs in the 1920s. They produced stylized portraiture, often with decorative backdrops, for British and American *Vogue*. Beaton's studio sets were theatrical masterpieces but, as with Steichen, the clothes took centre stage. Norman Parkinson, best known for his sophisticated, clean-cut images, was also to work for *Vogue* over the next two decades, before becoming a royal photographer in the 1950s.

Horst P. Horst was a highly regarded photographer of this era, known for his fashion silhouettes and portraits of society people and

for using studio lighting to dramatic effect. Man Ray was to take fashion photography one step further. Using specialized darkroom techniques he produced startling, innovative images that moved fashion photography into the realm of art.

The forties and fifties spawned new names such as Richard Avedon and Irving Penn, who brought a new, less static style of photography to the magazines. They went on to become two of photography's greatest legends. Penn is recognized for his strong, moody black and white images of women. In 1947, Irving Penn's *Twelve Most Photographed Models* was a tribute to the top models of his day. Richard Avedon's long career spans from the forties, when he was hired by *Harper's Bazaar* to photograph fashion models and celebrities. In the 1960s, Avedon moved to *Vogue* and continued to produce powerful images using contemporary models. Now in his seventies, he is still producing such great work as the celebrated 1995 Pirelli calendar and the evocative images of supermodels used for Gianni Versace's advertising campaigns.

The photography movement of the 1960s encapsulated a brand new mood. As fashion radically changed, photography became spontaneous, distorted and animated. David Bailey reshaped the image of models, by using scrawny, coltish females, such as the wide-eyed Jean Shrimpton and Penelope Tree to emphasize the freedom of this era.

Brian Duffy and Terence Donovan were two other photographers who captured the spirit of the sixties on film. Helmut Newton also emerged during this decade, and with his images of glamorous and erotic nudes, reflected the period's sexually liberated mood. Newton, whose work is still prominent today, is one of the most inspirational and imitated photographers of our time.

Herb Ritts made his name in the late seventies, having taken amateur photographers of his young actor friend Richard Gere. These photographs turned Gere into an object of desire and the former car salesman Ritts into a photography sensation.

Bruce Weber, who has become one of the greatest contemporary photographers, rose to prominence in the 1980s with his shots of male models. He also set a new trend with his black and white toned images. Arthur Elgort is another of photography's famous artists who has paid tribute to the many supermodels he has photographed in his *Model Manual*.

These celebrated names, along with today's leading photographers, whose stunning images appear on the pages of this book, are a collection of fashion photography's finest.

FASHION
DESIGNERS

Designers have played a major role in the rise of the supermodel. The designers are their mentors: they can hire, fire, make or break them.

Gianni Versace is applauded by his superbrigade of models.

Top designers hire models for their seasonal shows and fashion or fragrance advertising campaigns. Supermodels have become the ideal sales tools for the designers. They attract enormous press attention, irrespective of the outfit.

Gianni Versace was one of the first designers to use the supertroupe of Linda, Naomi, Christy and Cindy in his runway shows and advertising campaigns. Nowadays, to appear in one of Versace's campaigns can elevate a relatively unknown model to the upper echelons of supermodeldom. Karl Lagerfeld is one of the great fashion doyens who also has the power to turn models into superstars. Inès de la Fressange was one of the first models he built

into a star, when she became his muse for the house of Chanel. And when Claudia Schiffer succeeded her, she, too, reached superstar status. Calvin Klein is another prime model-maker who, along with leading international designers, has helped give models high-profile exposure. Here are some of the best.

AZZEDINE ALAÏA
Known as 'the king of cling', Azzedine Alaïa is one of the most influential French designers and a firm favourite of the supermodels. Alaïa is the only designer that the *crème de la crème* of supermodels will work for with payment in clothes instead of

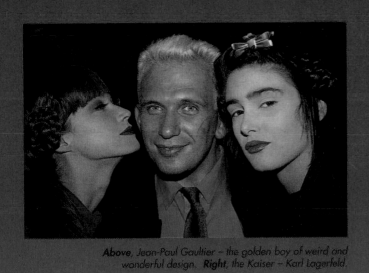

Above, Jean-Paul Gaultier – the golden boy of weird and wonderful design. *Right*, the Kaiser – Karl Lagerfeld.

money! He uses the finest quality fabrics to produce body-defining clothes designed to flatter and accentuate the female form. Best known for his dresses, Alaïa also works in leather and knitwear. Azzedine has many favourite supermodels, including Linda, Nadja, Christy, Kristen and Karen. But over the years he has built a special rapport with two models in particular – Naomi and Veronica. In 1995, he designed supermodel Stephanie Seymour's sensational wedding dress.

CALVIN KLEIN

Calvin Klein not only produces clothes and fragrances, but markets lifestyles. His range is compiled of sophisticated, minimalist basics: from jeans to underwear, casual sweats and sportswear. Klein started his own business in 1968, specializing in suits. By the mid-seventies, he had diversified into sports and casualwear. When he launched his range of underwear in 1983, women in their thousands bought his white, button-fly front briefs and boxer shorts. In 1986 Klein, who was one of the world's most eligible bachelors, married beautiful model Kelly Rector. She was his muse and his inspiration. Klein hires supermodels for his shows, apparel and fragrance campaigns. Christy, Amber and his number-one CK and *Obsession* muse, Kate Moss, are some of the supermodels that Klein has featured in his campaigns.

DOLCE & GABBANA

In 1985, the talented design duo of Domenico Dolce and Stefano Gabbana created one of fashion's most influential and prestigious labels. Their designs are expressive and directional, and represent a new generation of Italian design. In 1994, they launched a diffusion line – D & G. For their highly acclaimed shows they use such supermodels as Naomi, Helena, Kate, Yasmeen, Stella and Shalom. Linda has been a favourite for their main label advertising campaigns and Stella for D & G. Their clothes are not only popular among models and dedicated followers of fashion, but are also loved by celebrities, including Madonna, who ordered 1500 Dolce & Gabbana costumes for her *Girlie Show* tour.

DONNA KARAN

Donna Karan is a top American fashion designer who began her career working for Anne Klein. She soon became Klein's number two, and when Klein died in 1974, Karan became her successor.

By 1985, she had launched her own collection. During her time with Anne Klein she had worked closely with sportswear, which has greatly influenced her wearable designs. Her philosophy is to dress real women in comfortable, yet sassy clothes. DKNY, her highly successful younger and cheaper diffusion range, was launched in 1988. Donna Karan uses many of the supermodels for her seasonal shows held in New York. During one season however, she chose to use ordinary people rather than models on the runways!

GIANNI VERSACE

Gianni Versace is the king of Italian design. He creates extravagant, slinky numbers that are guaranteed to make an entrance, including the famous safety pin dress worn by actress and model Liz Hurley. Versace's shows are one of the highlights of the collections – attended by celebrities and VIP press, and presented by the entire brigade of the supermodel elite. He is known to hire the supermodels as he enjoys working with the best. His illustrious campaigns, photographed by the great maestros, have featured a band of superstar models, including Nadja, Kristen, Linda, Christy, Stephanie, Claudia and Stella. Gianni Versace started his career as a buyer for his mother's couture business, and launched his own collection in 1979. In addition to his main label and couture wear, Versace has two lower-priced lines Versus and Istante, along with his Versace Jeans couture label.

Above, mad about the boy – Giorgio Armani with his all-male showcast. **Right**, Fashion Queen Vivienne Westwood with Sarah Stockbridge.

GIORGIO ARMANI

Giorgio Armani has built a major fashion empire since starting his own business in 1973. His designs are often influenced by what his customers desire, with the individual being of far greater importance to Armani than current fads and theatrical gestures. His philosophy is to please the consumer by designing beautifully tailored clothes in top quality fabrics. In 1981 his empire expanded when he launched his younger label Emporio Armani, where you can sip a cappuccino while contemplating your purchases. Men's and women's apparel, jeans and accessories are sold worldwide through his state-of-the-art fashion emporiums. Armani has used an array of well-known models for his shows and advertising campaigns, including Linda, Christy, Karen, Yasmeen and Shalom.

GUCCI

Added to the list of ultra-fashionable collections, Gucci has, once again, become a favourite of fashion pundits, celebrities and models alike. Heather Stewart-Whyte, Kirsty Hume and Amber Valetta are the most recent Gucci campaign models but these supergirls will soon be superseded by virtual unknowns. Established in 1922 by Guccio Gucci as a saddlery shop, Gucci went on to become the epitome of chic, quality, Italian accessories. In 1993 the remaining member of the Gucci dynasty sold the empire to Investcorp. Meanwhile, a new American designer, Tom Ford, was hired to create a new clothing line and put the sparkle back into Gucci. And, if the responses to his last few collections of strong modern classics in rich shades and luxurious fabrics are anything to go by, he has succeeded beyond all expectation.

ISSEY MIYAKE

Issey Miyake is now a world-famous Japanese designer who, after studying design in Tokyo, moved to Paris to work as an assistant in the house of Guy Laroche. In 1970, after a short stint with Geoffrey Beene in New York, he launched his own collection. His garments are a blend of Japanese and European-influenced designs, incorporating original Japanese fabrics draped into geometric shapes. In 1973, he showed his first collection in Paris. Issey Miyake is renowned for using unconventional models in his shows – he recently hired five mature French actresses, one of whom was in her eighties. Eskimo model Irina is also a favourite of Miyake's.

JEAN-PAUL GAULTIER

After working for Pierre Cardin, French designer Jean-Paul Gaultier started up his own company in 1977, and has become one of the most directional designers of today. His collections are inspired by London's street style which, when fused with glamour, creates showy, alternative clothes. In 1988, he launched a successful younger label – Junior Gaultier – which was recently replaced by JPG, a cheaper, more sporty line than his main collection. Gaultier's showcast includes a bizarre mix of pop stars, old ladies, actresses and supermodels, including Nadja, Yasmeen, Eva and Kate.

JOHN GALLIANO

Models queue up to be in Galliano's shows. Kate, Helena, Naomi, Shalom and Amber are among some of the supermodels who have recently paraded around the stage in his spectacular performances. Galliano, who now operates from Paris, graduated from St Martins

School of Art in 1983. He is one of fashion's great geniuses and an undisputed British star. His clothes are a synchronicity of elegant couture wear and directional design. His biggest coup came in 1995, when he was approached by Hubert de Givenchy to succeed him as the House of Givenchy's new designer.

KARL LAGERFELD

Karl Lagerfeld, known as the Kaiser of fashion, is rarely seen without his props – a fan and dark glasses. Born in Hamburg in 1938, his love affair with fashion began when he moved to Paris in 1955 and became assistant to Pierre Balmain. He launched his first fragrance, *Chloé*, in 1975, and by 1983 had started working for Chanel, bringing an innovative new feel to Gabrielle Chanel's traditional designs. By 1984 he had founded his own company and was designing witty, imaginative garments for his Lagerfeld collection. Lagerfeld, who is also a talented photographer, uses a variety of supermodels to promote specific ranges: Claudia is his Chanel muse and he has recently used Kristen and Shalom in his advertising campaigns. Linda is his Chloé model, while Nadja represents the Lagerfeld collection. Helena and Trish are also current favourites.

PRADA

Prada's black nylon shopping bag has become synonymous with supermodels and fashion editors worldwide. This Italian company, run by Miuccia Prada, was founded as a leather goods company in 1913 by her grandfather. Since Miuccia staged her first collection of pure understated garments, invites to the show have become the hottest tickets in Milan. Prada is currently the label to be seen in – or carrying – as anyone who is anyone clutches a Prada bag. A new Prada and Miu Miu (her second label) collection is shown each fashion season, attracting the superstar models to its runway, including Nadja, Kristen and Carla, who have also appeared in Prada's campaigns.

VALENTINO

Valentino is a top Italian designer who, after working for almost ten years in Paris with Guy Laroche, opened his own couture house in Rome in 1959. He designs spectacular, opulent evening wear and elegant garments for an elite clientele. Valentino exhibited his very first collection in Rome in 1960. Since then, he has regularly shown his couture and ready-to-wear collections, as well as, more recently, his diffusion line, Oliver. Supermodels such as Linda, Helena, Carla and Karen can be seen on the runway wearing his elegant and sophisticated garments.

VIVIENNE WESTWOOD

Vivienne Westwood's spirited, dramatic and sometimes distorted designs are recognized worldwide. In 1971, she joined forces with Malcom McLaren to open her first shop, Let it Rock, in London's Kings Road. Their clothes attracted a great deal of attention and soon became an integral part of London's punk movement. Vivienne now has her own shop in the Kings Road called World's End. Vivienne is as eccentric as her designs, and caused a stir when she appeared on television wearing a totally transparent dress with only a fig leaf to cover her modesty. Her shows are theatrical extravaganzas. Her main muse for many years was model-turned-actress Sarah Stockbridge. Now Vivienne uses a selection of the supermodels, including Nadja, Helena, Karen, Kate, Eva and Shalom.

MAGAZINES

From the aspirational covers of the glossies to the directional, streetwise fashion stories of the style-press, models stare out at us from the covers and pages of every fashion magazine.

Today's fashion magazines offer an eclectic mix of fashion, beauty and culture. They are informative yet frivolous, inviting the reader to dip in and out of their pages and chew over the contents. Readers can discover the current fashions and be informed of recent make-up and beauty developments, as well as being kept up-to-date on movies, books and music. Some magazines have become more comprehensive and now cover a wider range of topics, such as controversial issues or current affairs features.

Over the last few years fashion magazines have become increasingly popular, selling more issues in each local market and expanding their international editions. *Elle* magazine now has twenty-five different editions worldwide. Many types of magazines are sold in the bookstalls under the heading of fashion magazines. These can be loosely divided into the following main categories.

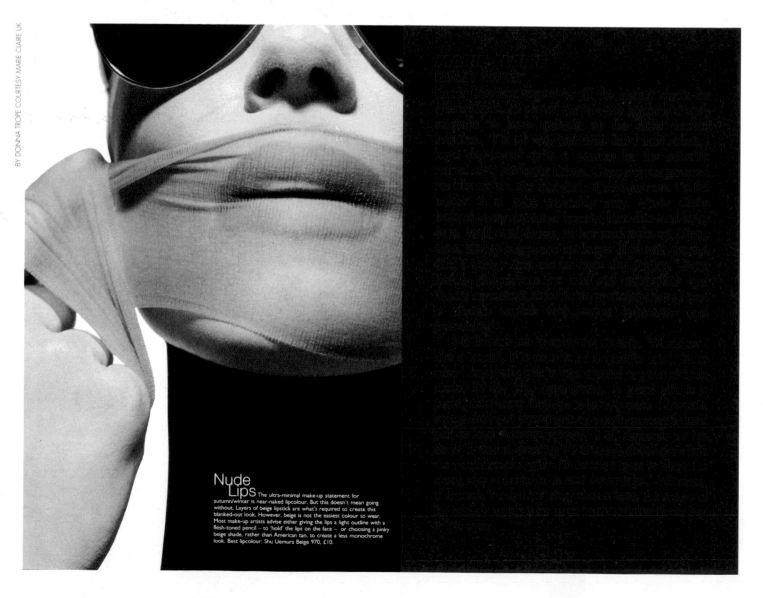

BY DONNA TROPF COURTESY MARIE CLAIRE UK

Nude Lips The ultra-minimal make-up statement for autumn/winter is near-naked lipcolour. But this doesn't mean going without. Layers of beige lipstick are what's required to create this blanked-out look. However, beige is not the easiest colour to wear. Most make-up artists advise either giving the lips a light outline with a flesh-toned pencil – to 'hold' the lips on the face – or choosing a pinky beige shade, rather than American tan, to create a less monochrome look. Best lipcolour: Shu Uemura Beige 970, £10.

HIGH FASHION MAGAZINES

There are only a handful of top international fashion magazines, such as *Vogue*, *Elle* and *Harper's Bazaar*, otherwise known as the glossies, or fashion bibles. These coffee-table journals are published monthly. They primarily feature top international designer clothes, although they do have special bargain sections, such as *Elle*'s 'Dress for Less' or *Vogue*'s 'Great Good Buys', which feature more affordable fashion. In keeping with their high profile, these magazines use premier-league supermodels along with the hottest rising stars. Their lavish fashion and beauty pages are illustrated with images by top fashion photographers. The cover price may be steep, but the product is an art form.

STYLE PRESS

Hip, trendy and often risqué: these magazines have a radical, hard-edged approach. Their fashion pages are filled with strong, off-beat imagery, and feature only the most directional designers, some with street appeal. They cover controversial topics and feature the grooviest bands and new releases; hottest clubs; current movies and, of course, the latest superbabe. Magazines on the cutting edge of style such as *The Face*, *Max*, *Interview*, *Details* and *Arena* are dual-purpose, read by both men and women, and bought by readers in their teens to late twenties. The style press often use supermodels on their covers, although they tend to choose strong, quirky-looking models for their fashion stories, in line with their style-led image.

FASHION/WOMEN'S MAGAZINES

These magazines feature fashion and beauty, but fulfil a slightly different role from that of high fashion magazines. Some, such as *Cosmopolitan*, aim to cover a number of women's topics including relationships and personal problems, as well as the usual reviews. They use more mainstream, commercial-looking models, although the more fashion-led publications often feature supermodels on their covers. The magazines within this market aim at different audiences: younger women who are more concerned with fashion and beauty; and the more mature woman who might be interested in cookery or decor.

VOGUE
FASHION BOOKINGS EDITOR

'It gives me a great sense of satisfaction to book a girl who is perfect for the story; or to book a new girl who goes on to make it big,' says Zoë Souter. As fashion bookings editor, Zoë is responsible for the production of *Vogue*'s fashion and beauty shoots. Nadja Auermann, pictured here, is one of the models she booked for a fashion story. It is also Zoë's job to book the photographers, hairstylists, make-up artists and assistants, as well as overseeing the travel arrangements for everyone involved and booking studios and locations.

Each day, Zoë liaises with bookers from model agencies around the world, arranging bookings for forthcoming shoots, and being updated on the movements of established models, as well as the hottest new faces. A large part of Zoë's day is spent seeing models and looking through their books. She will usually see around five girls a day. She then works closely with *Vogue*'s fashion editors and photographers to decide on the right model for each fashion story. Meanwhile, Zoë keeps a constant eye out for potentially fabulous new girls that might be suitable for *Vogue*. '*Vogue* models have to be modern, and look individual, intelligent and independent,' says Zoë.

ELLE
ASSOCIATE FASHION AND BEAUTY DIRECTOR

As associate fashion and beauty director, it is Kim's job to keep abreast of everything happening in the fashion and beauty industry. She must be aware of all the latest fashion trends, new shop openings, and fragrance or beauty product launches. Kim is in regular contact with the advertising and marketing departments, supplying them with the latest information so they are in a stronger position to pitch for advertising space. Protecting *Elle*'s commercial interests, Kim makes sure the fashion team features a wide range of designers. Her position also takes on a PR role: 'I arrange lunches between top designers and key people from the magazine, as well as hosting *Elle* reader events and keeping in close contact with the fashion PRs,' explains Kim.

After attending the seasonal shows, Kim edits *Elle*'s collections supplement. Here, she features a wide selection of catwalk shots, from the hottest designers, including her favourite – Helmut Lang, pictured here.

British *Elle* is one of the most directional fashion magazines. Consequently, they use many of the supermodels. 'We are not afraid to use up-and-coming models for our fashion shoots, but will only use major names such as Helena Christensen, Karen Mulder and Niki Taylor on the cover,' says Kim.

YOUTH/TEENAGE MAGAZINES

Aimed at the teenage market, magazines such as *Just Seventeen, Company, Miss Vogue,* and *Seventeen* combine fashion, music, film and often include posters of their readers' favourite pin-ups, such as models, and pop or movie stars. They are trivial, yet fun, and seem to achieve the blend that appeals to today's sophisticated teenagers. They hire young up-and-coming models, many of whom use these magazines as a launching-pad for their careers.

MEN'S FASHION MAGAZINES

Men's magazines have become popular with both men and women. Magazines such as *GQ* and *Esquire* cover a wide range of issues and include interviews with the hottest celebrity or personality, current affairs, the latest fashion and grooming pages and reviews. For their fashion pages they tend to use sophisticated male models with classic good looks rather than the off-beat alternative types. The female models they tend to hire, who are sometimes used in the fashion pages or on the covers, have a vampish, sex-kitten allure.

MAGAZINE PEOPLE

Labelled the fashion glitterati, fashionista or fashion mafia, magazine people are prime movers and shakers in the model industry. Unlike fashion designers and to some extent photographers, they are not well known outside the business, but on the modelling circuit they are some of fashion's most influential gurus.

It is the bookings editor, fashion editor and director who have the clout when it comes to choosing models. They are constantly on the lookout for new talent. Even if a model is relatively new and inexperienced, if she has the look of the moment or has been recommended by a top photographer, the magazine will use her.

There are a variety of editorial positions on magazines, from junior fashion assistant to editor. The structure and roles depend on the individual magazine, but generally consist of a fashion team of editors and directors, writers, stylists and assistants. Magazines also have an editor, publisher and beauty department. The fashion bibles such as *Vogue, Elle* and *Harper's Bazaar* also employ a bookings editor and associate fashion editor.

HARPER'S BAZAAR (USA)
FASHION ASSISTANT EDITOR

Naomi, Kate, Linda, Amber, Stella and Shalom – Lucy Sykes works with many of the supermodels. She is fashion assistant editor on *Harper's Bazaar* and also assists *Bazaar's* fashion director, Paul Cavaco. Aside from working for *Bazaar*, Lucy is also a freelance fashion stylist. *Harper's Bazaar* regularly use the premier-league supermodels, but do not rule out the up-and-coming models. They used Jodie Kidd at a very early stage of her career for one of their issues. *Harper's Bazaar* is one of the world's most highly-credited fashion bibles and is a showcase for work by such top photographers as Patrick Demarchelier and Peter Lindbergh.

For their fashion shoots the *Harper's Bazaar* team travel to exotic locations or work in studios in New York or Paris. Lucy spends most of her time either on shoots or preparing for them. "We usually shoot at least one day a week. Location shoots take longer and can last up to a few days," says Lucy. "On a typical day's shoot I arrive at the studio at 7am. The models arrive around 9.30 for hair and make-up which will often take until lunch time. During this time I make any necessary alterations to the clothes, by taking up hems or stitching any garments that are too big for the models. Once the shoot begins it is my job to make sure everything is absolutely perfect." Here is a result of one of her shoots – a cover of Linda Evangelista, photographed by Peter Lindbergh.

SKY
PUBLISHER

'One thing is clear from a magazine publishing viewpoint – as long as the supermodels are doing well, so are we,' says Steve Newbold, publisher of *Sky* magazine. As publisher, it is Steve's job to make sure each issue sells, and by placing a supermodel on the cover or producing supermodel posters or supplements he can be sure of an instant sell-out. 'Three of *Sky's* best-selling covers have been of Cindy Crawford, Elle Macpherson and Christy Turlington. And our supermodel supplement – *Models We Love*, which included Claudia, Kate, Linda, Naomi and Cindy – was one of the best-selling issues ever,' says Steve, pictured here with singer-actress Kylie Minogue at the 1994 British music industry ceremony, the Brit Awards.

Sky is a celebrity-driven magazine, but it is not only supermodels who adorn its covers and fill its pages. From Blur and Kylie Minogue to the members of the hippest new band, *Sky* is filled with pop stars, along with such movie stars as young Hollywood heart-throbs Christian Slater and Johnny Depp. *Sky* is read by both men and women and, as Steve points out, 'Men are clearly just as interested in supermodels as women!'

VOGUE (FRANCE)

FASHION EDITOR

Marie Amelie Sauvé is one of French *Vogue's* fashion editors. It is Marie Amelie's job to come up with a concept for each fashion story, such as a silent movie stars, space age theme or, pictured right, Karen Mulder in swinging sixties style. She works on one story per issue, planning it a month to six weeks ahead. 'We are working in advance all the time, which is crucial when it comes to booking models. If we do not allow plenty of time, the models we want for a particular shoot will not be available,' explains Marie Amelie. Once the model and photographer are booked and the clothes have been selected, Marie Amelie heads off to the studio to style the clothes and oversee the shoot. 'We use many different photographers, but at the moment I am working regularly with top Japanese photographer Satoshi Saikusa. As Satoshi prefers to shoot in a studio, very few of my shoots take place on location.'

Vogue has featured many of the supermodels. Karen Mulder, Carla Bruni, Kirsty Hume and Trish Goff are some of the models Marie Amelie has recently used. Each story is usually from eight to ten pages long, and features at least one model. Like British *Vogue*, French *Vogue* often uses new models that they feel have enormous potential. They have recently used rising star Jade Parfitt. This philosophy extends to the designers; Marie Amelie mixes new and lesser-known designers with well-known names.

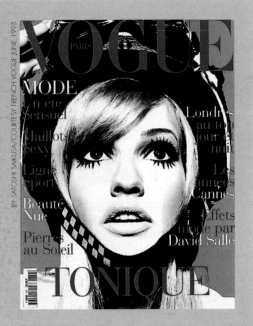

JAPANESE *ELLE*

EDITOR-IN-CHIEF/FASHION DIRECTOR

Elle is the only Japanese magazine to have western supermodels on its covers. Nadja, Eva, Claudia and Karen, pictured here, are regular cover girls. But for the inside of each issue, fifty per cent of the models Eriko Minamitani chooses are Japanese. Ayoko Harue, Eihi, Seiko and Kumiko are some of her favourites. 'I look for a strong character in a girl. She must not look remotely ordinary or boring, and must have a directional, modern image. Many Japanese girls have baby faces and look too young, so I tend to choose twenty to twenty-five year olds who have a mature look about them,' says Eriko.

Most of Japanese *Elle's* fashion and beauty pages are shot in Japan by Japanese photographers, but occasionally, if they are working on a special project, Eriko and her team will come to Europe. As fashion director, Eriko also travels to Europe for the collections, or to interview famous designers, like Yohji Yamamoto or Issey Miyake. 'Like western magazines we use a mix of international designers such as Jean Paul Gaultier, John Galliano and Prada, as well as the Japanese designers,' explains Eriko. Eriko's job is split into two major roles. Aside from running the fashion department as editor-in-chief she oversees the entire magazine. This is a cover from one of the issues Eriko edited.

TO ALL MODELS *Catwalk* is a tribute to supermodels. We would have loved to feature many more models, but due to lack of space we were prevented from doing so. All models featured are in alphabetical order with a mixture of megamodels and supermodels in the full page and half page sections.

PHOTOGRAPHIC CREDITS Jacket credits: *Left* Nadja Auermann at the A/W 94/95 Blumarine show, *Centre* Naomi Campbell at the A/W 94/95 Chanel show and *Right* Helena Christensen at the A/W 94/95 Richard Tyler show. Photographed by and with great thanks to © Niall McInerney. A very special thank you to all the following photographers and magazines. 1, 2, 7, 9 top, 13 bottom, 21, 32 top, 35 bottom, 36 top, 37 top, 39 top, 44, 45, 47 bottom, 62, 67, 71 small picture, 72, 73, 74, 75 top, 78, 79, 80, 81, 82, 83, 84, 85, 86, 88, 89, 90, 91: courtesy of © Niall McInerney. Endpaper: Sante D'Orazio courtesy *Vogue*, © Condé Nast Publications Ltd. 4: courtesy Pamela Hanson. 6 top: Peter Lindbergh courtesy *Vogue*, © Condé Nast Publications Ltd. 6 bottom: courtesy Rex USA. 8 top: courtesy Abiaw. 8 centre: courtesy Nils Jorgensen. 8 bottom: courtesy Peter Brooker. 9 centre: courtesy Express Newspapers Ltd. 9 bottom: courtesy *The Times*. 10: Irving Penn for American *Vogue*, courtesy *Vogue* (UK), © Condé Nast Publications Ltd. 11: Cecil Beaton courtesy *Vogue*, © Condé Nast Publications Ltd. 12 top: courtesy Hulton Deutsch. 12 bottom: courtesy Express Newspapers. 13 top: Cecil Beaton courtesy *Vogue*, © Condé Nast Publications Ltd. 14: Neil Kirk courtesy *Vogue*, © Condé Nast Publications Ltd. 15: Kelly Klein courtesy *Vogue*, © Condé Nast Publications Ltd. 16 & 17: Peter Lindbergh courtesy © *Harper's Bazaar*. 18: courtesy Mark Hom/*Sky Magazine*. 19: courtesy Gilles Bensimon/*Elle* Portugal. 20: Uli Weber courtesy © *Elle* UK. 22: Regan Cameron courtesy © *Elle* UK. 23: Sante D'Orazio/courtesy *Allure*, copyright © Condé Nast Publications Inc. 24: Huggy/courtesy Elite Premier, *Elle* Hong Kong. 25: Nick Knight courtesy *Vogue*, © Condé Nast publications Ltd. 26: Patrick Demarchelier courtesy © *Harper's Bazaar*. 27: Mark Liddell courtesy © *Elle* UK. 28: Richard Imrie courtesy *Tatler*, © Condé Nast publications Ltd. 29: Sante D'Orazio courtesy *Vogue*, © Condé Nast Publications Ltd. 30: Peggy Sirota courtesy © *Elle* UK. 31 top: Nick Knight courtesy *Vogue*, © Condé Nast Publications Ltd. 31 bottom: Michael Thompson/courtesy *Mademoiselle*, copyright © Condé Nast Publications Inc. 32 bottom: courtesy Monic Richard/*Elle* Quebec. 33 top: courtesy Robert Erdmann/*Marie Claire* Italy. 33 bottom: courtesy François Rotger/*Harpers & Queen*. 34 top: courtesy André Rau/*Elle* France. 34 bottom: courtesy Francesco Scavullo/*Cosmopolitan* USA. 35 top: Hiromasa courtesy © *Marie Claire* UK. 36 bottom: Patrick Demarchelier courtesy © *Harper's Bazaar*. 37 bottom: courtesy Christian Witkin/Sygma/*W*. 38 top: Christophe Kutner courtesy © *Elle* UK. 38 bottom: Uli Weber courtesy © *Donna* magazine. 39 bottom: Manuela Pavesie courtesy *Vogue*, © Condé Nast publications Ltd. 40 top: Mark Liddell courtesy © *Marie Claire* UK. 40 bottom: Regan Cameron courtesy *Vogue*, © Condé Nast publications Ltd. 41 top: courtesy Marc Hispard/*Elle* France. 41 bottom: Mark Liddell courtesy © *Marie Claire* UK. 43: courtesy Marco Glaviano. 47 top: Jose Aragon courtesy Models 1. 47 centre: Justin Smith courtesy Elite Premier. 48: J.R. Duran courtesy *Tatler*, © Condé Nast publications Ltd. 49: Troy Word courtesy © *Marie Claire* UK. 50: courtesy Bruce Weber/Abercrombie & Fitch. 51: courtesy Guiba Guimaraes. 52: courtesy Gilles Bensimon/*Elle* USA. 53: courtesy Brian Nice/*Marie Claire* Japan (May 1994). 54 & 55: courtesy Alan Strutt/*ES* magazine. 56: courtesy Adrian Green/*Just Seventeen*. 57: courtesy Juergen Teller. 58: Josh Vangelder courtesy © *Donna* magazine. 59: Stephanie Pfriender courtesy © *Elle* UK. 60 & 61 courtesy Rod Howe. 63 top: courtesy Perfect Picture. 63 bottom: courtesy Pamela Hanson. 64 top: courtesy Peter Lindbergh/*Harper's Bazaar*. 64 bottom left: courtesy Michael Thompson/*Vogue* France, Condé Nast S.A. 64 bottom right: Regan Cameron courtesy © *Elle* UK. Both Linda Evangelista's portfolio and Karen Mulder's card with thanks to Elite Premier Tel: 0171 333 0888. 65 large picture: Regan Cameron courtesy *Vogue*, © Condé Nast Publications Ltd. 65 small picture: courtesy *Vogue*, © Condé Nast Publications Ltd. 66: courtesy Patrick Demarchelier/Revlon. 68 & 69: courtesy Rod Howe. 70: courtesy Sipa. 71 large picture: Sante D'Orazio courtesy *Vogue*, © Condé Nast Publications. 75 bottom: Sante D'Orazio courtesy *Vogue*, © Condé Nast Publications Ltd. 77: Neil Kirk courtesy *Vogue*, © Condé Nast Publications Ltd. 87: courtesy Richard Young. 92: Donna Trope courtesy © *Marie Claire* UK. 93 top: Jacques Olivier courtesy *Vogue*, © Condé Nast publications Ltd. 93 bottom: Charlotte Macpherson courtesy © *Elle* UK. 94 top: Peter Lindbergh courtesy © *Harper's Bazaar*. 94 bottom: courtesy Steve Newbold. 95 top: courtesy Satoshi Saikusa/*Vogue* France (June 1995), Condé Nast S.A. 95 bottom left: courtesy André Rau/*Elle* Japan. 95 bottom right: courtesy Stephanie Stevens. Every effort has been made to ensure that the credits are accurate. However, if any errors are brought to the attention of the publishers, they will be more than happy to make any corrections in the event of a reprint.

ACKNOWLEDGEMENTS The author would like to say a very special thank you to all the models featured, and to the following people in the model and fashion industries who so kindly gave their time and information, or quotations for *Catwalk*. A very special thanks to Chris Owen, Lisa Smith, Sophie Wood and Millie at Elite Premier, Tel: 0171-333 0888, Elite House, 40-42 Parker St, London WC2; Paula Karaiskos and Sarah Doukas at Storm, Tel: 0171-352 2278, 1st Floor, 5 Jubilee Place, London SW3; April Ducksbury, Tori Lloyd-Edwards, Nigel and Karen Ford at Models 1, Tel: 0171-351 7107, Omega House, 471-473 Kings Road, London SW10; Michelle Anderson and Sarah Leon at Select Models, Tel: 0171-470 5200, 3rd Floor, 43 King Street, London WC2; Elaine Noble and Jonathan Phang at IMG, Tel: 0171-486 8011, 13-16 Jacob's Well Mews, George St, London W1; Brad Parson at Boss Models, Tel: 0171-580 2444, 7 Berners Mews, London W1; Pauline Bernatchez and Bradley Young at Pauline's, 379 W. Broadway, New York, NY 10012, USA; Melissa Richardson at 2 Management, Tel: 0171-836 4501; Annette Russell at So Dam Tuff; Neal and Nadine Johnson at Ford New York; Corinne Nicolas at Elite New York; Jennifer Borak and Stuart Cameron at Women. A very big thank you to Zoë Souter, Lucinda Chambers, Plum Sykes and Claire Grant at *Vogue* UK; Kim Stringer, Duane Ashurst and Tomo Delaney at *Elle* UK; Emma Bannister and Mel Brodie at *Marie Claire*; Steve Newbold at *Sky*; Stephanie Stevens at *Just Seventeen*; Lucy Sykes and Lauren E. Purcell at *Harper's Bazaar*; Marie Amelie Sauvé at French *Vogue*; Eriko Minamitani at Japanese *Elle*. A very special thanks to Maggie Hunt, Mary Greenwell, Ruby Hammer, Sam McKnight, Terence Renatti, Emma Bannister and Rob Lander for their quotes for make-up, hair, beauty and superhints; also to Storm, Elite Premier, IMG and Select for their models' superhints; and Nicky Clarke, Charlie Duffy and Colin Gold, for their superhints. Thank you especially to to Karl Lagerfeld, Gianni Versace, John Galliano, Azzedine Alaïa, Leslie Kark at Lucie Clayton, Pamela Hanson, Corinne Day and George Fellows at Revlon for their quotes, and to all their PRs for the information. Sandra would like to say how grateful she is to her editor Richard Atkinson and publisher Michael Dover at Weidenfeld & Nicolson and her agent Fiona Batty for turning her dream into reality, to Rochelle Visick for her help clearing permissions, and a special thank you to Richard for his support throughout the book's creation. She would also like to extend her gratitude by saying a special thanks to Dan and Nicola for their support during the frantic summer spent working on *Catwalk*.